CLARENDON ARISTOTLE SERIES

General Editors

J. L. ACKRILL AND LINDSAY JUDSON

D1520781

Also published in this series

Categories and *De Interpretatione*
J. L. ACKRILL

De Generatione et Corruptione
C. J. F. WILLIAMS

De Partibus Animalium I and *De Generatione Animalium* I
D. M. BALME
New impression with supplementary material by Allan Gotthelf

Eudemian Ethics Books I, II, and VIII
MICHAEL WOODS
Second edition

Metaphysics Books Γ, Δ, and E
CHRISTOPHER KIRWAN
Second edition

Metaphysics Books M and N
JULIA ANNAS

Physics Books I and II
WILLIAM CHARLTON
New impression with supplementary material

Physics Books III and IV
EDWARD HUSSEY
New impression with supplementary material

Posterior Analytics
JONATHAN BARNES
Second edition

Other volumes are in preparation

ARISTOTLE
DE ANIMA

BOOKS II AND III

(WITH PASSAGES FROM BOOK I)

*Translated
with Introduction and Notes
by*

D. W. HAMLYN

*With a Report on Recent Work
and a Revised Bibliography
by*

CHRISTOPHER SHIELDS

CLARENDON PRESS · OXFORD
1993

Oxford University Press, Walton Street, Oxford OX2 6DP

Oxford New York Toronto
Delhi Bombay Calcutta Madras Karachi
Kuala Lumpur Singapore Hong Kong Tokyo
Nairobi Dar es Salaam Cape Town
Melbourne Auckland Madrid

and associated companies in
Berlin Ibadan

Oxford is a trade mark of Oxford University Press

Published in the United States
by Oxford University Press Inc., New York

First published 1968; reprinted six times
Reprinted with new material 1993

British Library Cataloguing in Publication Data
Data available

Library of Congress Cataloging in Publication Data
De anima: books II and III with passages from book 1/Aristotle; translated with
introduction and notes by D. W. Hamlyn; with a report on recent work and a revised
bibliography by Christopher Shields.
Includes bibliographical references and index.
1. Psychology—Early works to 1800. I. Hamlyn, D. W., 1924– II. Shields,
Christopher John. III. Title. IV. Series
B415.A5H28 1993 128—dc20 93–18647
ISBN 0-19-824084-8 ISBN 0-19-824085-6 (pbk.)

1 3 5 7 9 10 8 6 4 2

Printed in Great Britain
on acid-free paper by
Biddles Ltd, Guildford and King's Lynn

PREFACE

I MUST express my debt to Professor J. L. Ackrill, the editor of the series, for his great help in the preparation of this book. He has read with patience and thoroughness the drafts which I have produced, and has made a host of invaluable suggestions. He has thereby saved me from a number of serious errors and has prompted me to make many improvements both in the translation and in the notes. I am greatly indebted to him. Such errors as remain are entirely my own responsibility.

I am also conscious of my debt to colleagues in the University of London, especially those who took part in a seminar on *De Anima III* at the Institute of Classical Studies, London, during 1962 and 1963. I owe a special debt in this respect to Professor D. J. Furley, Dr. A. R. Lacey, Professor B. A. O. Williams, and Professor J. S. Wilkie. I have no doubt absorbed many of their ideas, often without realizing it, and I make due acknowledgement of this. My thanks are also due to Professor P. G. Winch for comments on the Introduction.

I am very grateful to Mrs. Susan Cunnew for her great help in typing the manuscript and for advice and assistance in other ways in preparing the final version of the book. Finally, I must express my thanks to my daughter, Catherine, for her enthusiastic help in checking the typescript.

D. W. HAMLYN

Birkbeck College

EDITORS' NOTE

We are grateful to Professor Shields for undertaking the preparation of the report on recent work and the revised bibliography.

J.L.A.
R.L.J.

March 1993

CONTENTS

INTRODUCTION

ARISTOTLE'S *De Anima* is often referred to as Aristotle's psychology. This is not a very accurate description of it, as there is comparatively little psychology in it in the modern sense of the word. There is a certain amount of physiology and in many sections the emphasis is definitely biological, involving, as elsewhere in Aristotle, considerable emphasis on teleology. But the great bulk of the discussion is concerned with 'philosophy of mind'. That is to say that Aristotle is concerned to elucidate the nature and role of the concepts necessary for an understanding of the mind or, more generally, of the soul (for the notion of the *mind* was to the Greeks a more limited one than it is for us, being confined to the more intellectual aspects of the mental life). In this, his point of origin is commonly held beliefs on the matter—a procedure which makes his inquiry, in his own terms, a dialectical one. In this respect his approach to the soul is like his approach to nature in general, in the *Physics*. In neither work is his point of origin the empirical facts as such, as opposed to the common beliefs referred to. The same reasons which make it appropriate to say that Aristotle is concerned in the *Physics* with the philosophy of nature rather than physics in the modern sense make it right to say that in the *De Anima* he is concerned not with psychology but the philosophy of mind or soul.

Aristotle starts from the principle which runs through most of earlier Greek thought—that the soul, whatever else it is, is the principle of life, i.e. that which makes living things alive, and is responsible, in some sense, for

the different living functions. Thus his approach to his
subject-matter is that of one concerned with general
forms of life, i.e. the general capacities and potentialities
which living things possess. It is this approach which
determines his account of the soul as the form of a living
body, or, more precisely, 'the first actuality of a natural
body which has organs' (the 'first actuality' being a
special sort of potentiality, a *hexis*, which is actual in
comparison with the potentialities of non-living things).
In other words, to speak of the soul is to speak of the
potentialities which a living thing has for different forms
of life. If this view of the matter seems so different from
that of Plato (it takes no account, for example, of the
problems of personal immortality with which Plato was
concerned), it takes its starting-point, in the way indicated,
from the most common Greek conception of the 'psyche'
and works out the implications of this.

The main question which arises is whether Aristotle's
conceptual apparatus is sophisticated enough for the
purposes for which it is intended. To this the answer is,
I believe, 'No'. The notion of *actuality* which Aristotle
employs serves, as will be seen from the notes, to distinguish the potentialities which a living thing has from the
potentialities for movement or change possessed by
inanimate bodies, but it does no more than this. The
notion is thus descriptive or classificatory, but it is not
explanatory. What Aristotle does in this respect is to try
to distinguish living things from inanimate things and to
give a descriptive account of forms of life, summed up in
a few schematic concepts like those of 'potentiality', 'activity', 'actuality', and 'being affected'. Indeed the conceptual scheme involved is a remarkably simple one. The
manifestations of life are all thought of as forms of change,
or, to be more accurate, the actualization of various

potentialities. These potentialities constitute the various faculties—those of nutrition and reproduction, perception, and thought (with imagination and locomotion fitted in somehow). These are all things which a living thing of one kind or another can do or has the potentiality for doing (though not every living thing, of course, can do all of them). Moreover, Aristotle thinks that they form a hierarchy such that the higher functions are dependent on the lower.

By far the greatest amount of space is given over to perception, and the intellect is treated in a way which is almost parallel to the way in which perception is treated. Aristotle's account of perception is in many ways in line with those of his predecessors, especially the Presocratics. He starts from the idea that in perception a sense-organ is affected in some way, that changes are caused in it by things around us. But he adds refinements to this notion. He says that in sense-perception the sense-organ receives the form of the object without its matter; the object actualizes a potentiality which the organ has for receiving forms of objects, so that the sense-organ becomes what the object is. Before perception the sense-organ is potentially what the object is actually (and this too provides a refinement on the idea that like affects like and a reconciliation between it and the idea that unlike affects unlike). These refinements are such that Aristotle can come to say in III. 7 (and the remark is echoed elsewhere) that perception is not a case of being affected at all. Along with this, however, Aristotle also speaks of the role of judgement in perception—that in perception we pass judgement on objects, that we discriminate between them and so on. The emphasis on judgement seems to become greater in Book III, perhaps owing to the fact that he also considers there the intellect and the part that judgement plays in this; the parallel between the senses and the intellect makes him put greater emphasis than before on the role of judgement in the former.

Despite all this, the general account of sense-perception remains for the most part basically physiological. This raises problems for the parallel account of the intellect, which, he thinks, has no special organ, and cannot for this reason be treated physiologically. The fact that Aristotle can persist in maintaining the parallelism between the senses and the intellect casts some obscurity on his account of the latter. On the other hand, there is much in his account which remains essentially philosophical, e.g. the account of the relations between the senses and their different kinds of object, and his account of the 'common sense'. Aristotle is intent not just to give the physiological basis of perception, but to understand what perception, the senses, etc., are; and the same goes for the other faculties. But if this approach is philosophical, there is little in it which is epistemological in the traditional sense. Aristotle has little interest in attempts to justify the claim of the senses to provide knowledge, and his account contains practically nothing of the paraphernalia of such attempts—the appeal to sense-data and the like. His account is elucidatory rather than justificatory. This is not in any way a criticism of Aristotle; quite the contrary. It is the understanding of the concepts of perception, etc., which should be the primary aim of philosophy in this field. The scepticism which underlies the demands for justification arises most often from misunderstandings concerning these concepts.

On the other hand, certain philosophical problems receive less than satisfactory treatment.

(1) There is little in the *De Anima* on the subject of the emotions or feelings in general. They are mentioned but

almost completely undiscussed; for Aristotle's account of the emotions we have to turn to the *Rhetoric*, Bk. II.

(2) Aristotle's dealings with the traditional mind–body problem are perfunctory. He assumes in general that his concern is with functions which are those of both body and soul. Indeed this must be so, given his account of the soul as the form of the body. But there is an almost total neglect of any problem arising from psycho-physical dualism and the facts of consciousness. Such problems do not seem to arise for him. The reason appears to be that concepts like that of consciousness do not figure in his conceptual scheme at all; they play no part in his analysis of perception, thought, etc. (Nor do they play any significant role in Greek thought in general.) It is this perhaps that gives his definition of the soul itself a certain inadequacy for the modern reader. It is true, of course, that he sometimes behaves as if there were a clear distinction between the soul and the body; he speaks of certain functions as being functions of the soul and he speaks, at any rate in one passage in Book I, of a movement reaching the soul or starting from it, thus suggesting that the soul has something of a life of its own and that there are psychical processes in their own right apart from bodily ones. But his main ostensible point is that psychical processes are processes of *living* things; it is the distinction between the living and non-living which receives the main emphasis in his thought, not the traditional mind–body distinction which has been developed since his day.

(3) Connected with the previous point is the fact that he gives little attention to the role of the concepts of a person, the subject of consciousness and personal identity. Despite a remark in Book I that it would be better to say that the *man* does things like pitying, learning, and thinking with his soul, rather than that the soul itself does these, Aristotle

rarely lives up to his dictum. The lack of concepts of this kind emerges quite definitely in his treatment of what is in effect the problem of self-consciousness in III. 2. But it is also evident in the fact that there is no real discussion of action in the *De Anima*. There is a discussion of movement, which stresses the role of desire and the imagination as factors in this, but this scarcely adds up to an account of action as such. What Aristotle chiefly has in mind are the causal conditions of movement, and his lack of a proper concept of a person or of consciousness makes a proper account of action impossible. (For an action is something performed by a person, and the connexions between the concepts of action and intention imply also the idea that a person must sometimes be aware of what he is doing.)

In sum, while Aristotle does discuss faculties like those of nutrition and locomotion, the larger part of his account of the functions of the soul is devoted to those functions which play an epistemological role, i.e. to perception and thought, although his own interest in them is not itself epistemological. Imagination has an unsatisfactory half-way status in his scheme between perception and the intellect, and its exact position is never made clear. After the account of the intellect (puzzling as it is) the discussion tails off, and despite a brief account of locomotion much of the rest of the work is fragmentary. It is perception in its various forms which remains the main interest, and despite Aristotle's attempts to arrive at an understanding of this, that understanding is largely chained to the tradition from which Aristotle's account stems—that of physiological or causal accounts of perception.

Thus while Aristotle's work is notable as that of perhaps the first philosopher to deal systematically with the philosophy of mind—the first to attempt systematically to elucidate the concepts necessary for an understanding of human and animal mental functions—it is limited in scope. Its limitations are added to by the inadequacies referred to above, in the conceptual scheme with which Aristotle approaches his subject. Nevertheless, with the *De Anima* Aristotle can be said to have founded the 'philosophy of mind'; the book is the first systematic attempt to provide an understanding of those functions which may be called 'mental', as well as those which are more general functions of living things. In this respect, Aristotle's account has, and will continue to have, a certain fascination.

The structure of the *De Anima* is that it begins typically in Book I with an attempt to set the stage, largely by a review of past opinions on the subject. (The majority of these discussions of past thought on the subject are not included in the present translation. The parts which are included are those which lay down the problems to be dealt with and which reflect on later discussions in the other books.) Book II and at least the first half of Book III constitute the substantive treatment of the issues, but Book III tails off into a number of chapters which deal, not always consistently, with separate issues. It is possible that Chapter 6 of Book III ends the main fabric of the work, although Chapters 9, 10, and possibly 11—the treatment of movement—should probably be put with it. Some of the rest looks extraneous to the main fabric, although it may constitute in part notes on that main fabric. The last two chapters appear in some ways closer to the *Parva Naturalia* than they do to the rest of the *De Anima*. The relation between the *De Anima* and the *Parva Naturalia* is a much disputed matter. The latter collection of works is perhaps more biological in tone and has more truck with technicality of a biological or physiological kind. If one thing is noticeable about the *De Anima* it is its general refusal to adopt technicality or technical language. When Aristotle makes certain distinctions in the *De Anima* or uses the conceptual apparatus which he has developed elsewhere, he tends in a number of instances to explain or illustrate this, and does not have recourse to special technical language. This is less typical of the *Parva Naturalia*, and one senses a difference of purpose behind the works. There is, as indicated, evidence of technical knowledge in the *Parva Naturalia* which is missing in the *De Anima*. On the other hand, the latter has, to my mind, a general sophistication of thought which is not present in the *Parva Naturalia*, and while it is impossible to be certain about the matter, I suspect that the *De Anima* is the more mature work.

NOTES ON THE TRANSLATION

ARISTOTLE has the reputation of being a philosopher with a largely technical vocabulary. That is to a great extent true. On the other hand, some of his key-terms have, as we should put it, an essential ambiguity, which Aristotle treats, in virtue of his theory of meaning, as having philosophical significance. His treatment of *ousia* (οὐσία—substance/essence), for example, is well known for its importance for his general metaphysics. This particular term figures, but not largely, in the *De Anima*. I have drawn attention to other terms in the notes. There are, however, certain terms which require mention here:

(1) *Logos* (λόγος): this term necessitates a wide range of translations, as its sense varies from 'definition' (as a set of words), via what I have translated not altogether happily as 'principle' (something objective which determines a thing's nature), to 'proportion'. I have not sought to achieve uniformity of translation, but to prevent misunderstanding I have flagged all occurrences of the word by providing the translations with the subscript '$_L$'.

(2) Certain terms connected with perception:

(*a*) *Aisthēsis* (αἴσθησις): This may be translated variously as 'sense', 'perception', perhaps 'sensation', etc., and is sometimes used even to refer to the sense-organ. I have flagged all of its occurrences with the subscript '$_A$' (*v.* also the notes on 413^{b}4).

(*b*) Terms constructed from verbs of perception, etc., with an article and the termination '-*ikos*', the most

xvii

common form being that with the neuter definite article, e.g. *to aisthētikon* (τὸ αἰσθητικόν). These should literally be translated 'that which can perceive', etc., and I have tried to translate them in this way wherever possible. In such cases, the term may refer to the animal, a sense-organ, the soul or a part of it. In some cases, either because the above procedure would result in excessive awkwardness or because it is obvious that one is supposed to supply some such phrase as 'part of the soul', I have had resort to other translations, including that most commonly used by translators—'faculty'. I have, however, flagged all occurrences of the construction by the subscript '$_K$' (*v.* also the notes on 413^{b}4). (In consequence, also, I have translated *dunamis* (δύναμις) as 'potentiality' throughout, and never as 'faculty', despite some cases of awkwardness.)

(*c*) The two occurrences of *aisthēma* (αἴσθημα) I have noted by indicating the Greek word.

(*d*) I have tried to translate *to aisthēton* (τὸ αἰσθητόν) and its variants as 'object of perception' throughout, again despite some cases of awkwardness.

(*e*) The *idia* (ἴδια) and *koina* (κοινά) introduced in II. 6 I have translated in their subsequent occurrences as 'special-objects' and 'common-objects' respectively, treating them as technical terms.

The text used is that of the Oxford Classical Text (ed. W. D. Ross). I have noted a number of variant readings which I have adopted. I have used the normal conventions for bracketing doubtful readings, i.e. square brackets for proposed deletions and diamond brackets for proposed additions. I have also occasionally used { . . . } brackets to indicate places where certain crucial words have to be supplied.

PASSAGES FROM BOOK I
RELEVANT TO THE ARGUMENT
IN BOOKS II AND III

CHAPTER 1

402ª1. Knowledge we regard as a fine and worth-while thing, and one kind as more so than another either in virtue of its accuracy or in virtue of its being concerned with superior and more remarkable things. On both these grounds we should with reason place the study of the soul in the first rank. It would seem, also, that an acquaintance with it makes a great contribution to truth as a whole, and especially to the study of nature; for the soul is as it were the first principle of animal life. We seek to inquire into and ascertain both its nature and its essence, and after that all the attributes belonging to it; of these some are thought to be properties peculiar to the soul, while others are thought to belong because of it to animals also.

402ª10. But in every respect and in every way it is the most difficult of things to attain any conviction about it. For, since the inquiry is common to many other things too—I mean that concerning essence and what a thing is— it might perhaps be thought that there is one procedure in the case of all those things for which we wish to ascertain the essence, just as there *is*, demonstration, for the incidental properties; so that we ought to look for this procedure. But if there is not one common procedure for dealing with what a thing is, the undertaking will be still more difficult; for we shall have to establish what is

the way to proceed in each case. And if it is evident
whether this consists in demonstration or division or some
other procedure, there will still be many puzzles and
uncertainties as to what starting-points we must use in our
inquiry; for different subjects, e.g. numbers and planes,
have different first principles.

402ª23. First surely we must determine in which of the
genera the soul is and what it is; I mean whether it is a
particular thing and substance or quality or quantity or
some other of the categories which have been distinguished.
And secondly we must determine whether it is one of those
things which are in potentiality or whether it is rather
a kind of actuality; for this makes no small difference.
And we must inquire also if it is divisible or indivisible
and whether every soul is of like kind or not; and if not
of like kind, whether differing in species or genus.

402ᵇ3. For as things are, people who speak and inquire
about the soul seem to study the human soul only. But we
must take care not to overlook the question whether there
is one definition_L of the soul, as of animal, or whether
there is a different one for each, as of horse, dog, man, and
god, the universal animal being either nothing or secon-
dary; and it would be similar for any other common
predicate.

402ᵇ9. Furthermore, if there are not many souls but only
parts, should we inquire into the whole soul or its parts?
It is difficult too to decide which of these are really
different from each other, and whether we must inquire
into the parts first or their functions, e.g. thinking or the
intellect, and perceiving or that which can perceive_K;
and similarly for the rest also. And if the functions come

2

first, the question might be raised whether we should inquire into the corresponding objects before these, e.g. the object of perception before that which can perceive$_K$, and the object of thought before the intellect.

402^{b}16. It seems that not only is ascertaining what a thing is useful for a consideration of the reasons for the attributes which follow upon essences (as in mathematics ascertaining what straight and curved or line and surface are is useful for seeing to how many right angles the angles of a triangle are equal), but also conversely the attributes contribute a great part to the knowledge of what a thing is; for when we are able to give an account of either all or most of the attributes as they appear to us, then we shall be able to speak best about the essence too; for the starting-point of every demonstration is what a thing is, so that, for those definitions which do not enable us to ascertain the attributes nor even make it easy to guess about this, it is clear that they have all been stated dialectically and to no purpose.

403ª3. There is also the problem whether the properties of the soul are all common also to that which has it or whether any are peculiar to the soul itself; for it is necessary to deal with this, though it is not easy. It appears that in most cases the soul is not affected nor does it act apart from the body, e.g. in being angry, being confident, wanting, and perceiving in general; although thinking looks most like being peculiar to the soul. But if this too is a form of imagination or does not exist apart from imagination, it would not be possible even for this to exist apart from the body.

403ª10. If then there is any of the functions or affections of the soul which is peculiar to it, it will be possible for it to be separated from the body. But if there is nothing peculiar to it, it will not be separable, but it will be like the straight, to which, *qua* straight, many properties belong, e.g. it will touch a bronze sphere at a point, although the straight if separated will not so touch; for it is inseparable, if it is always found with some body.

403ᵃ16. It seems that all the affections of the soul involve the body—passion, gentleness, fear, pity, confidence, and, further, joy and both loving and hating; for at the same time as these the body is affected in a certain way. This is shown by the fact that sometimes when severe and manifest sufferings befall us we are not provoked to exasperation or fear, while at other times we are moved by small and imperceptible sufferings when the body is aroused and is as it is when it is in anger. This is even further evident; for men may come to have the affections of the frightened although nothing frightening is taking place.

403ᵃ24. If this is so, it is clear that the affections {of the soul} are principles$_L$ involving matter. Hence their definitions are such as 'Being angry is a particular movement of a body of such and such a kind, or a part or potentiality of it, as a result of this thing and for the sake of that'. And for these reasons an inquiry concerning the soul, either every soul or this kind of soul, is at once the province of the student of nature.

403ᵃ29. But the student of nature and the dialectician would define each of these differently, e.g. what anger is. For the latter would define it as a desire for retaliation or something of the sort, the former as the boiling of the blood and hot stuff round the heart. Of these, the one gives the matter, the other the form and principle$_L$. For this is the principle$_L$ of the thing, but it must be in a matter of such and such a kind if it is to be. Thus the principle$_L$ of a house is, say, that it is a covering to prevent destruction by winds, rain, and heat, but someone else will say that a house is stones, bricks, and timber, and another again that it is the form in them for the sake of these other things.

403^{b}7. Which of these, then, is the student of nature? Is it the one who is concerned with the matter, but is ignorant of the principle$_L$, or the one who is concerned with the principle$_L$ only? Or is it rather the one who is concerned with the product of both? Who then is each of the others? Or is there no particular person who is concerned with the properties of matter which are not separable nor treated as separable, while the student of nature is concerned with everything which is a function or affection of such and such a body and such and such a matter? Anything not of this kind is the concern of someone else, and in some cases of a craftsman perhaps, e.g. a carpenter or doctor. The properties which are not separable, but which are not treated as properties of such and such a body but in abstraction, are the concern of the mathematician. Those which are treated as separable are the concern of the 'first philosopher'.

403^{b}16. Let us return to the point from which our discussion$_L$ began. We were saying that the affections of the soul are, at any rate in so far as they are such ⟨as⟩ passion and fear, inseparable in this way[1] from the natural matter of the animals in which they occur, and not in the same way as a line or surface.

---

[1] The text is uncertain here. Ross's addition of οἷα seems plausible. The reading οὔτως ἀχώριστα—'inseparable in this way'—is less certain, but the general sense of the passage is clear enough.

CHAPTER 4

408ª34. . . . . There will be greater reason for raising the question whether the soul is moved, on consideration of the following. We say that the soul is grieved, rejoices, is confident and afraid, and again is angry, perceives, and thinks. And all these seem to be movements. One might conclude from this that the soul itself is moved; but this is not necessary.

408ᵇ5. Even if it is indeed the case that being grieved, rejoicing, and thinking are movements, that each of them consists in being moved, and that the movement is due to the soul, e.g. that being angry and being afraid consist in the heart's being moved in a particular way and that thinking is a movement either of this perhaps or of some other part, and that some of these happen because of movements in place and others because of movements constituting alteration (what sort and how is a matter for a separate discussion$_L$)—then to say that the soul is angry is as if one were to say that the soul weaves or builds. For it is surely better not to say that the soul pities, learns, or thinks, but that the man does these with his soul; and this not because the movement takes place in it, but because sometimes it reaches as far as it or at other times comes from it; e.g. perception$_A$ starts from particular things, while recollection starts from the soul itself and extends to movements or persistent states in the sense-organs.

408ᵇ18. The intellect seems to be born in us as a kind of substance and not to be destroyed. For it would be destroyed if at all by the feebleness of old age, while as things are what happens is similar to what happens in the case of the sense-organs. For, if an old man acquired an eye

6

of a certain kind, he would see as well as even a young man. Hence old age is not due to the soul's being affected in a certain way, but to this happening to that which the soul is in, as is the case in drunkenness and disease.

408ᵇ24. Thus thought and contemplation decay because something else within is destroyed, while thought is in itself unaffected. But thinking and loving or hating are not affections of that, but of the individual thing which has it, in so far as it does. Hence when this too is destroyed we neither remember nor love; for these did not belong to that, but to the composite thing which has perished. But the intellect is surely something more divine and is unaffected. . . .

CHAPTER 5

410ᵃ23. . . . It is absurd too to say that the like is unaffected by the like, and yet that like perceives like and knows the like by the like. Yet they assert that perceiving is a form of being affected and moved; and similarly for thinking and knowing. . . .

BOOK II

CHAPTER 1

412ᵃ3. Enough has been said of the views about the soul which have been handed down by our predecessors. Let us start again, as it were from the beginning, and try to determine what the soul is and what would be its most comprehensive definition$_L$.

412ᵃ6. Now we speak of one particular kind of existent things as substance, and under this heading we so speak of one thing *qua* matter, which in itself is not a particular, another *qua* shape and form, in virtue of which it is then spoken of as a particular, and a third *qua* the product of these two. And matter is potentiality, while form is actuality—and that in two ways, first as knowledge is, and second as contemplation is.

412ᵃ11. It is bodies especially which are thought to be substances, and of these especially natural bodies; for these are sources of the rest. Of natural bodies, some have life and some do not; and it is self-nourishment, growth, and decay that we speak of as life. Hence, every natural body which partakes of life will be a substance, and substance of a composite kind.

412ᵃ16. Since it is indeed a body of such a kind (for it is one having life), the soul will not be body; for the body is not something predicated of a subject, but exists rather as subject and matter. The soul must, then, be substance *qua* form of a natural body which has life potentially.

8

Substance is actuality. The soul, therefore, will be the actuality of a body of this kind.

412ᵃ22. But actuality is so spoken of in two ways, first as knowledge is and second as contemplation is. It is clear then that the soul is actuality as knowledge is; for both sleep and waking depend on the existence of soul, and waking is analogous to contemplation, and sleep to the possession but not the exercise of knowledge. In the same individual knowledge is in origin prior. Hence the soul is the first actuality of a natural body which has life potentially.

412ᵃ28. Whatever has organs will be a body of this kind. Even the parts of plants are organs, although extremely simple ones, e.g. the leaf is a covering for the pod, and the pod for the fruit; while roots are analogous to the mouth, for both take in food.

412ᵇ4. If then we are to speak of something common to every soul, it will be the first actuality of a natural body which has organs. Hence too we should not ask whether the soul and body are one, any more than whether the wax and the impression are one, or in general whether the matter of each thing and that of which it is the matter are one. For, while unity and being are so spoken of in many ways, that which is most properly so spoken of is the actuality.

412ᵇ10. It has then been stated in general what the soul is; for it is substance, that corresponding to the principle_L of a thing. And this is 'what it is for it to be what it was' for a body of such a kind. Compare the following: if an instrument, e.g. an axe, were a natural body, then its substance would be what it is to be an axe, and this would be its soul; if this were removed it would no longer be an axe, except homonymously. But as it is it

9

is an axe; for it is not of this kind of body that the soul is 'what it is for it to be what it was' and the principle_L, but of a certain kind of natural body having within itself a source of movement and rest.

412ᵇ17. We must consider what has been said in relation to the parts of the body also. For, if the eye were an animal, sight would be its soul; for this is an eye's substance—that corresponding to its principle_L. The eye is matter for sight, and if this fails it is no longer an eye, except homonymously, just like an eye in stone or a painted eye. We must now apply to the whole living body that which applies to the part; for as the part is to the part, so analogously is perception_A as a whole to the whole perceptive body as such.

412ᵇ25. It is not that which has lost its soul which is potentially such as to live, but that which possesses it. Seeds and fruit are potentially bodies of this kind.

412ᵇ27. Just, then, as the cutting and the seeing, so too is the waking state actuality, while the soul is like sight and the potentiality of the instrument; the body is that which is this potentially. But just as the pupil and sight make up an eye, so in this case the soul and body make up an animal.

413ᵃ3. That, therefore, the soul or certain parts of it, if it is divisible, cannot be separated from the body is quite clear; for in some cases the actuality is of the parts themselves. Not that anything prevents at any rate *some* parts from being separable, because of their being actualities of no body. Furthermore, it is not clear whether the soul is the actuality of the body in the way that[1] the sailor is of the ship. Let this suffice as a rough definition and sketch about the soul.

----

[1] Deleting the ἤ which Ross adds to the text.

CHAPTER 2

413ª11. Since it is from things which are obscure but more obvious that we arrive at that which is clear and more intelligible in respect of the principle$_L$ involved, we must try again in this way to treat of the soul; for a defining statement$_L$ should not only make clear the fact, as the majority of definitions do, but it should also contain and reveal the reason for it. As things are, the statements$_L$ of the definitions are like conclusions. For example, what is squaring? The construction of an equilateral rectangle equal to one which is not equilateral. But such a definition is a statement$_L$ of the conclusion; whereas one who says that squaring is the discovery of the mean proportional states the reason for the circumstance.

413ª20. We say, then, making a beginning of our inquiry, that that which has soul is distinguished from that which has not by life. But life is so spoken of in many ways, and we say that a thing lives if but one of the following is present—intellect, perception$_A$, movement, and rest in respect of place, and furthermore the movement involved in nutrition, and both decay and growth.

413ª25. For this reason all plants too are thought to live; for they evidently have in them such a potentiality and first principle, through which they come to grow and decay in opposite directions. For they do not grow upwards without growing downwards, but they grow in both directions alike and in every direction—this being so of all that are constantly nourished and continue to live, as long as they are able to receive nourishment. This {form of life} can exist apart from the others, but the others cannot exist apart from it in mortal creatures. This is obvious in the case of plants; for they have no other potentiality of soul.

413ᵇ1. It is, then, because of this first principle that living things have life. But it is because of sense-perception$_A$ first of all that they will be animal, for even those things which do not move or change their place, but which do have sense-perception$_A$, we speak of as animals and not merely as living.

413ᵇ4. First of all in perception$_A$ all animals have touch. Just as the nutritive faculty$_K$ can exist apart from touch and from all sense-perception$_A$, so touch can exist apart from the other senses$_A$. We speak of as nutritive that part of the soul in which even plants share; all animals clearly have the sense$_A$ of touch. The reason for each of these circumstances we shall state later.

413ᵇ11. For the present let it be enough to say only that the soul is the source of the things above mentioned and is determined by them—by the faculties of nutrition$_K$, perception$_K$, thought$_K$, and by movement. Whether each of these is a soul or a part of a soul, and if a part, whether it is such as to be distinct in definition$_L$ only or also in place, are questions to which it is not hard to find answers in some cases, although others present difficulty.

413ᵇ16. For, just as in the case of plants some clearly live when divided and separated from each other, the soul in them being actually one in actuality in each plant, though potentially many, so we see this happening also in other varieties of soul in the case of insects when they are cut in two; for each of the parts has sense-perception$_A$ and motion in respect of place, and if sense-perception$_A$, then also imagination and desire. For where there is sense-perception$_A$, there is also both pain and pleasure, and where these, there is of necessity also wanting.

413ᵇ24. Concerning the intellect and the potentiality for contemplation the situation is not so far clear, but it seems to be a different kind of soul, and this alone can exist separately, as the everlasting can from the perishable.

413ᵇ27. But it is clear from these things that the remaining parts of the soul are not separable, as some say; although that they are different in definition$_L$ is clear. For being able to perceive and being able to believe are different, since perceiving too is different from believing; and likewise with each of the other parts which have been mentioned.

413ᵇ32. Moreover, some animals have all these, others only some of them, and others again one alone, and this will furnish distinctions between animals; what is the reason for this we must consider later. Very much the same is the case with the senses$_A$; for some animals have them all, others only some, and others again one only, the most necessary one, touch.

414ᵃ4. That by means of which we live and perceive is so spoken of in two ways, as is that by means of which we know (we so speak in the one case of knowledge, in the other of soul, for by means of each of these we say we know). Similarly, we are healthy in the first place by means of health and in the second by means of a part of the body or even the whole. Now, of these knowledge and health are shape and a kind of form and principle$_L$, and as it were activity of the recipient, in the one case of that which is capable of knowing$_K$, in the other of that which is capable of health (for the activity of those things which are capable of acting$_K$ appears to take place in that which is affected and disposed). Now the soul is in the primary

13

way that by means of which we live, perceive, and think.
Hence it will be a kind of principle$_L$ and form, and not
matter or subject.

414ª14. Substance is so spoken of in three ways, as we have
said, and of these cases one is form, another matter, and
the third the product of the two; and of these matter is
potentiality and form actuality. And since the product of
the two is an ensouled thing, the body is not the actuality
of soul, but the latter is the actuality of a certain kind of
body.

414ª19. And for this reason those have the right conception
who believe that the soul does not exist without a body
and yet is not itself a kind of body. For it is not a body,
but something which belongs to a body, and for this
reason exists in a body, and in a body of such and such
a kind. Not as our predecessors supposed, when they fitted
it to a body without any further determination of what
body and of what kind, although it is clear that one
chance thing does not receive another. In our way it
happens just as reason$_L$ demands. For the actuality of each
thing comes naturally about in that which is already such
potentially and in its appropriate matter. From all this it
is clear that the soul is a kind of actuality and principle$_L$
of that which has the potentiality to be such.

CHAPTER 3

414ª29. Of the potentialities of the soul which have been
mentioned, some existing things have them all, as we
have said, others some of them, and certain of them only
one. The potentialities which we mentioned are those for
nutrition$_K$, sense-perception$_K$, desire$_K$, movement$_K$ in
respect of place, and thought$_K$.

414^{a}32. Plants have the nutritive faculty$_K$ only; other creatures have both this and the faculty of sense-perception$_K$. And if that of sense-perception$_K$, then that of desire$_K$ also; for desire comprises wanting, passion, and wishing: all animals have at least one of the senses$_A$, touch, and for that which has sense-perception$_A$ there is both pleasure and pain and both the pleasant and the painful: and where there are these, there is also wanting: for this is a desire for that which is pleasant.

414^{b}6. Furthermore, they have a sense$_A$ concerned with food;[1] for touch is such a sense$_A$; for all living things are nourished by dry and moist and hot and cold things, and touch is the sense$_A$ for these[1] and only incidentally of the other objects of perception; for sound and colour and smell contribute nothing to nourishment, while flavour is one of the objects of touch. Hunger and thirst are forms of wanting, hunger is wanting the dry and hot, thirst wanting the moist and cold; and flavour is, as it were, a kind of seasoning of these. We must make clear about these matters later, but for now let us say this much, that those living things which have touch also have desire.

414^{b}16. The situation with regard to imagination is obscure and must be considered later. Some things have in addition the faculty of movement$_K$ in respect of place, and others, e.g. men and anything else which is similar or superior to man, have that of thought$_K$ and intellect.

414^{b}20. It is clear, then, that it is in the same way as with figure that there will be one definition$_L$ of soul; for in the former case there is no figure over and above the triangle

---

[1] Removing the brackets to be found in the O.C.T., which imply a different interpretation.

and the others which follow it in order, nor in the latter case is there soul over and above those mentioned. Even in the case of figures there could be produced a common definition$_L$, which will fit all of them but which will not be peculiar to any one. Similarly too with the kinds of soul mentioned.

414^{b}25. For this reason it is foolish to seek both in these cases and in others for a common definition$_L$, which will be a definition$_L$ peculiar to no actually existing thing and will not correspond to the proper indivisible species, to the neglect of one which will.

414^{b}28. The circumstances with regard to soul are similar to the situation over figures; for in the case both of figures and of things which have soul that which is prior always exists potentially in what follows in order, e.g. the triangle in the quadrilateral on the one hand, and the nutritive faculty$_K$ in that of perception$_K$ on the other. Hence we must inquire in each case what is the soul of each thing, what is that of a plant, and what is that of a man or a beast.

414^{b}33. For what reason they are so arranged in order of succession must be considered. For without the nutritive faculty$_K$ there does not exist that of perception$_K$; but the nutritive faculty$_K$ is found apart from that of perception$_K$ in plants. Again, without the faculty of touch$_K$ none of the other senses$_A$ exists, but touch exists without the others; for many animals have neither sight nor hearing nor sense$_A$ of smell. And of those which can perceive$_K$, some have the faculty of movement$_K$ in respect of place, while others have not. Finally and most rarely, they have reason and thought; for those perishable creatures which have reason have all the rest, but not all those which have each of the others have reason. But some do not even have imagination, while others live by this alone. The contemplative intellect requires a separate discussion$_L$. That the account, therefore, appropriate for each of these is most appropriate for the soul also is clear.

CHAPTER 4

415^{a}14. Anyone who is going to engage in inquiry about these must grasp what each of them is and then proceed to investigate what follows and the rest. But if we must say what each of them is, e.g. what is the faculty of thought$_K$ or of perception$_K$ or of nutrition$_K$, we must again first say what thinking and perceiving are; for activities and actions are in respect of definition$_L$ prior to their potentialities. And if this is so, and if again, prior to them, we should have considered their correlative objects, then we should for the same reason determine first about them, e.g. about nourishment and the objects of perception and thought.

415^{a}22. Hence, we must first speak about nourishment and reproduction; for the nutritive soul belongs also to the other living things and is the first and most commonly possessed potentiality of the soul, in virtue of which they all have life. Its functions are reproduction and the use of food; for it is the most natural function in living things, such as are perfect and not mutilated or do not have spontaneous generation, to produce another thing like themselves—an animal to produce an animal, a plant a plant—in order that they may partake of the everlasting and divine in so far as they can; for all desire that, and for the sake of that they do whatever they do in accordance with nature. (But that for the sake of which is twofold—the purpose for which and the beneficiary for whom.) Since, then, they cannot share in the everlasting and divine by continuous existence, because no perishable thing can persist numerically one and the same, they share in them in so far as each can, some more and some less; and what persists is not the thing itself but something like itself, not one in number but one in species.

$415^{b}8$. The soul is the cause and first principle of the living body. But these are so spoken of in many ways, and similarly the soul is cause in the three ways distinguished; for the soul is cause as being that from which the movement is itself[1] derived, as that for the sake of which it occurs, and as the essence of bodies which are ensouled.

$415^{b}12$. That it is so as essence is clear; for essence is the cause of existence for all things, and for living things it is living that is existing, and the cause and first principle of this is the soul. Furthermore, the actuality is the principle$_L$ of that which is such potentially.

$415^{b}15$. And it is clear that the soul is cause also as that for the sake of which. For just as the intellect acts for the sake of something, in the same way also does nature, and this something is its end. Of this sort is the soul in animals in accordance with nature; for all natural bodies are instruments for soul, and just as it is with those of animals so it is with those of plants also, showing that they exist for the sake of soul. But that for the sake of which is so spoken of in two ways, the purpose for which and the beneficiary for whom.

$415^{b}21$. Moreover, soul is also that from which motion in respect of place is first derived; but not all living things have this potentiality. Alteration and growth also occur in virtue of soul; for perception$_A$ is thought to be a kind of

---

[1] Reading αὐτή with most MSS.

alteration, and nothing perceives which does not partake of soul. And the situation is similar with growth and decay; for nothing decays or grows naturally unless it is nourished, and nothing is nourished which does not share in life.

415^b28. Empedocles did not speak well when he added this, that growth takes place in plants, when they root themselves downwards because earth naturally moves in this direction, and when they grow upwards because fire moves in that way. For he does not have a good understanding of up and down (for up and down are not the same for all things as they are for the universe, but the roots of plants are as the head in animals, if we are to speak of organs as different or the same in virtue of their functions). In addition to this, what is it that holds together the fire and the earth, given that they tend in opposite directions? For they will be torn apart, unless there is something to prevent them; but if there is, then this is the soul and the cause of growth and nourishment.

416^a9. Some think that it is the nature of fire which is the cause quite simply of nourishment and growth; for it appears that it alone of bodies [or elements] is nourished and grows. For this reason one might suppose that in both plants and animals it is this which does the work. It is in a way a contributory cause, but not the cause simply; rather it is the soul which is this. For the growth of fire is unlimited while there is something to be burnt, but in all things which are naturally constituted there is a limit and a proportion$_L$ both for size and for growth; and these belong to soul, but not to fire, and to principle$_L$ rather than to matter.

416^a19. Since it is the same potentiality of the soul which is nutritive and reproductive, we must first determine the facts about nutrition; for it is distinguished in relation to the other potentialities by this function. It is thought that one thing is food for its contrary, though not in all cases, but wherever contraries receive not only generation from each other but also growth; for many things come to be from each other, but not all are quantities, e.g. the healthy comes to be from the sick. Not even those which do receive growth from each other seem to constitute food for each other in the same way; but water is food for fire, while fire does not feed water. It seems, then, that it is especially in the simple bodies that one thing is food, the other the thing fed.

416ª29. But there is a difficulty here; for some say that the like is fed by like, as is the case with growth, while others, as we have said, think the reverse, that one thing is fed by its contrary, since the like is unaffected by like whereas food changes and is digested; and in all cases change is to the opposite or to an intermediate state. Furthermore, food is affected by that which is fed, but not the latter by the food, just as the carpenter is not affected by his material, but the latter by him; the carpenter changes merely from idleness to activity.

416ᵇ3. It makes a difference whether the food is the last thing which is added or the first. But if both are food, but the one undigested and the other digested, it would be possible to speak of food in both ways; in so far as the food is undigested, the opposite is fed by opposite, in so far as it is digested, the like by like. So that it is clear that in a way both speak rightly and not rightly.

416ᵇ9. But since nothing is fed which does not partake of life, that which is fed would be the ensouled body, *qua* ensouled, so that nourishment too is relative to that which is ensouled, and this not accidentally.

416ᵇ11. But being food and being capable of producing growth are different; for it is in so far as the ensouled thing is something having quantity that food is capable of producing growth, but it is in so far as it is a particular and a substance that it is food. For the ensouled thing maintains its substance and exists as long as it is fed; and it can bring about the generation not of that which is fed, but of something like it; for its substance is already in existence, and nothing generates itself, but rather maintains itself. Hence this first principle of the soul is a potentiality such as to maintain its possessor as such, while food prepares it for activity; for this reason, if deprived of food it cannot exist.

416ᵇ20. Since there are three things, that which is fed, that with which it is fed, and that which feeds, that which feeds is the primary soul, that which is fed is the body which has this, and that with which it is fed is the food.

416ᵇ23. Since it is right to call all things after their end, and the end is to generate something like oneself, the primary soul will be that which can generate something like itself.

416ᵇ25. That with which one feeds is twofold, just as that with which one steers is, i.e. both the hand and the rudder, the one moving and being moved, the other being moved only. Now it is necessary that all food should be capable of being digested, and it is heat which effects the digestion; hence every ensouled thing has heat. What nourishment is has now been stated in outline; but we must elucidate it later in the appropriate work$_L$.

CHAPTER 5

416ᵇ32. Now that these matters have been determined let us discuss generally the whole of perception$_A$. Perception$_A$ consists in being moved and affected, as has been said; for it is thought to be a kind of alteration. Some say too that the like is affected by like. How this is possible or impossible we have stated in our general account$_L$ of acting and being affected.

417ᵃ2. There is a problem why perception$_A$ of the senses$_A$ themselves does not occur, and why they do not give rise to perception$_A$ without there being any external objects, although there is in them fire, earth, and the other elements, of which, either in themselves or in respect of their accidents, there is perception$_A$. It is clear, then, that the faculty of sense-perception$_K$ does not exist by way of activity but by way of potentiality only; for this reason the perception does not occur, just as fuel does not burn in and through itself without something that can burn it; otherwise it would burn itself and would need no actually existing fire.

417ᵃ9. Since we speak of perceiving in two ways (for we speak of that which potentially hears and sees as hearing and seeing, even if it happens to be asleep, as well as of that which is actually doing these things); perception$_A$ too will be so spoken of in two ways, the one as in potentiality, the other as in actuality. Similarly with the object of perception too, one will be potentially, the other actually.

417ᵃ14. First then let us speak as if being affected, being moved, and acting are the same thing; for indeed movement is a kind of activity, although an incomplete one, as has been said elsewhere. And everything is affected and moved by something which is capable of bringing this about and is in actuality. For this reason, in one way, as we said, a thing is affected by like, and in another by unlike; for it is the unlike which is affected, although when it has been affected it is like.

417ᵃ21. But we must make distinctions concerning potentiality and actuality; for at the moment we are speaking[1] of them in an unqualified way. For there are knowers in that we should speak of a man as a knower because man is one of those who are knowers and have knowledge; then there are knowers in that we speak straightaway of the man who has knowledge of grammar as a knower. (Each of these has a capacity but not in the same way—the one because his kind, his stuff, is of this sort, the other because he can if he so wishes contemplate, as long as nothing external prevents him.) There is thirdly the man who is already contemplating, the man who is actually and in the proper sense knowing this particular A. Thus, both the first two, ⟨being⟩ potential knowers, ⟨become actual knowers⟩, but the one by being altered through learning and frequent changes from an opposite disposition, the other by passing in another way from the state of having arithmetical or grammatical knowledge without exercising it to its exercise.

417ᵇ2. Being affected is not a single thing either; it is first a kind of destruction of something by its contrary, and second it is rather the preservation of that which is so potentially by that which is so actually and is like it in the way that a potentiality may be like an actuality. For that which has knowledge comes to contemplate, and this is

---

[1] Reading λέγομεν with MSS. Torstrik's emendation ἐλέγομεν accepted by the O.C.T. is clearly unnecessary.

either not an alteration (for the development of the thing is into itself and into actuality) or a different kind of alteration. For this reason it is not right to say that something which understands is altered when it understands, any more than a builder when he builds. The leading of a thinking and understanding thing, therefore, from being potentially such to actuality should not be called teaching, but should have another name; while that which, starting from being potentially such, learns and acquires knowledge by the agency of that which is actually such and is able to teach either should not be said to be affected, as has been said, or else we should say that there are two kinds of alteration, one a change to conditions of privation, the other to a thing's dispositions and nature.

417ᵇ16. The first change in that which can perceive$_K$ is brought about by the parent, and when it is born it already has sense-perception in the same way as it has knowledge. Actual sense-perception is so spoken of in the same way as contemplation; but there is a difference in that in sense-perception the things which are able to produce the activity are external, i.e. the objects of sight and hearing, and similarly for the rest of the objects of perception. The reason is that actual perception$_A$ is of particulars, while knowledge is of universals; and these are somehow in the soul itself. For this reason it is open to us to think when we wish, but perceiving is not similarly open to us; for there must be the object of perception. The situation is similar with sciences dealing with objects of perception, and for the same reason, that objects of perception are particular and external things.

417ᵇ29. But there will be an opportunity later to clarify these matters; for the present let it be enough to have determined this much—that, while that which is spoken of as potential is not a single thing, one thing being so spoken of as we should speak of a boy as a potential general, another as we should so speak of an adult, it is in the latter way with that which can perceive$_K$. But since the difference between the two has no name, although it has been determined that they are different and how they are so, we must use 'to be affected' and 'to be altered' as though they were the proper words.

418ᵃ3. That which can perceive$_K$ is, as we have said, potentially such as the object of perception already is actually. It is not like the object, then, when it is being affected by it, but once it has been affected it becomes like it and is such as it is.

CHAPTER 6

418ᵃ7. We must speak first of the objects of perception in relation to each sense$_A$. But objects of perception are so spoken of in three ways; of these we say that we perceive two in themselves, and one incidentally. Of the two, one is special to each sense$_A$, the other common to all.

418ᵃ11. I call special-object whatever cannot be perceived by another sense$_A$, and about which it is impossible to be deceived, e.g. sight has colour, hearing sound, and taste flavour, while touch has many varieties of object. But at any rate each judges about these, and is not deceived as to the fact that there is colour or sound, but rather as to what or where the coloured thing is or as to what or where the object which sounds is.

418ᵃ16. Such then are spoken of as special to each, while those that are spoken of as common are movement, rest, number, figure, size; for such as these are not special to any, but common to all. For certain movements are perceptible by both touch and sight.

418ª20. An object of perception is spoken of as incidental, e.g. if the white thing were the son of Diares; for you perceive this incidentally, since this which you perceive is incidental to the white thing. Hence too you are not affected by the object of perception as such.

418ª24. Of the objects which are perceived in themselves it is the special-objects which are objects of perception properly, and it is to these that the essence of each sense$_A$ is naturally relative.

CHAPTER 7

418ª26. That of which there is sight, then, is visible. What is visible is colour and also something which may be described in words$_L$, but happens to have no name; what we mean will be clear as we proceed. For the visible is colour, and this is that which overlies what is in itself visible—in itself visible not by definition$_L$, but because it has in itself the cause of its visibility. Every colour is capable of setting in motion that which is actually transparent, and this is its nature. For this reason it is not visible without light, but the colour of each thing is always seen in light.

418ᵇ3. Hence we must first say what light is. There is, surely, something transparent. And I call transparent what is visible, not strictly speaking visible in itself, but because of the colour of something else. Of this sort are air, water, and many solid bodies; for it is not *qua* water or *qua* air that these are transparent, but because there exists in them a certain nature which is the same in them both

and also in the eternal body above. Light is the activity of
this, the transparent *qua* transparent. Potentially, wherever
this is, there is darkness also. Light is a sort of colour of
the transparent, when it is made actually transparent by
fire or something such as the body above; for to this too
belongs something which is one and the same.

418ᵇ13. What then the transparent is and what light is has
been stated, i.e. that it is not fire nor body generally, nor
an effluence from any body (for it would be a body in that
case also), but the presence of fire or something of that
kind in the transparent. For it is impossible for two bodies
to be in the same place at the same time, light is thought
to be the opposite of darkness, and since darkness is the
privation of such a disposition from the transparent, it is
clear that the presence of this is light.

418ᵇ20. Empedocles, and anyone else who maintained the
same view, was wrong in saying that light travels and
arrives[1] at some time between the earth and that which
surrounds it, without our noticing it. For this is contrary
to the clear evidence of reason$_L$ and also to the apparent
facts; for it might escape our notice over a short distance,
but that it does so over the distance from east to west is
too big an assumption.

418ᵇ26. It is the colourless which is receptive of colour,
and the soundless of sound. And it is the transparent
which is colourless, as is also the invisible or barely visible,
as dark things seem to be. The transparent is of this kind,
not when it is actually transparent, but when it is potentially so; for the same nature is sometimes darkness and
sometimes light.

[1] Reading γιγνομένου with most MSS.

419ª1. Not everything is visible in light, but only the colour proper to each thing; for some things are not seen in the light but bring about perception$_A$ in the dark, e.g. those things which appear fiery and shining (and there is no one name for them), such as fungus, horn,[1] the heads, scales, and eyes of fish; but in none of these is the proper colour seen.

419ª6. The reason why these things are seen requires separate discussion$_L$. This much is clear for now, that what is seen in light is colour. For this reason too it is not seen without light; for this is just what it is to be colour, to be capable of setting in motion that which is actually transparent; and the actuality of the transparent is light. There is a clear indication of this; for if one places that which has colour upon the eye itself, one will not see it. In fact, the colour sets in motion the transparent, e.g. air, and the sense-organ is moved in turn by this when it is continuous.

419ª15. For Democritus did not speak rightly, thinking that if the intervening space were to become a void, then even if an ant were in the sky it would be seen accurately; for this is impossible. For seeing takes place when that which can perceive$_K$ is affected by something. Now it is impossible for it to be affected by the actual colour which is seen; it remains for it to be affected by what is intervening, so that there must be something intervening. But if it were to become a void, not only should we not see accurately, but nothing would be seen at all.

419ª22. The reason why colour must be seen in the light has been stated. Fire is seen both in darkness and in light, and this is necessarily so; for the transparent becomes transparent through it. The same account$_L$ applies to both

---

[1] Or possibly 'flesh', if the suggested emendation κρέας be adopted.

sound and smell. For none of these produces sense-perception$_A$ when it touches the sense-organ, but the intervening medium is moved by smell and sound, and each of the sense-organs by this in turn. And when one puts the sounding or smelling object on the sense-organ, it produces no perception$_A$. The same applies to touch and taste, though it is not obvious; the reason why will be clear later. The medium for sounds is air, that for smell has no name. For there is a quality common to air and water, and this, which is present in both, is to that which has smell as the transparent is to colour; for even animals which live in water appear to have perception$_A$ of smell. But man and those land-animals which breathe cannot smell unless they breathe. The reason for these things too will be studied later.

CHAPTER 8

419^{b}4. Let us now first determine the facts about sound and hearing. Sound exists in two ways; for there is sound which is something in actuality, and sound which is so potentially. For some things we say do not have a sound, e.g. sponge or wool, while others do, e.g. bronze and anything solid and smooth, because they can make a sound, that is they can produce an actual sound between themselves and the organ of hearing.

419^{b}9. Actual sound is always of something in relation to something and in something; for it is a blow which produces it. For this reason it is impossible for there to be sound when there is only one thing; for the striker and the thing struck are different. Hence the thing which makes the sound does so in relation to something; and a blow cannot occur without movement. But, as we have said, sound is not the striking of any chance thing; for wool produces no sound if it is struck, but bronze does, and any smooth and hollow object. Bronze does so because it is smooth, while hollow objects produce many blows after the first by reverberation, that which is set in motion being unable to escape.

419ᵇ18. Furthermore, sound is heard in air, and also in water although less so, but it is not the air or the water which is responsible for the sound; rather, there must be solid objects striking against each other and against the air. This happens when the air remains after being struck and is not dispersed. For this reason it makes a sound if it is struck quickly and forcibly; for the movement of the striker must be too quick for the air to disperse, just as if one[1] were to strike a blow at a heap or whirl of sand in rapid motion.

419ᵇ25. An echo occurs when the air is made to bounce back like a ball from air which has become a single mass on account of a container which has limited it and prevented it from dispersing. It is likely that an echo always occurs, although not a distinct one, since the same thing surely happens with sound as with light too; for light is always reflected (otherwise there would not be light everywhere, but there would be darkness outside the area lit by the sun), but it is not reflected as it is from water, or bronze, or any other smooth object, so as to produce a shadow, by which we delimit the light.

419ᵇ33. The void is rightly said to be responsible for hearing. For the air is thought to be a void, and it is this which produces hearing, when it is moved as a single, continuous mass. But, because of its lack of coherence, it makes no

---

[1] Reading τις with MSS.

noise, unless that which is struck is smooth. Then the air becomes a single mass at the same time, because of the surface of the object; for a smooth object has a single surface.

420ª3. It is, then, that which can move air which is single because continuous as far as the organ of hearing which can produce sound. Air is naturally one with the organ of hearing; and because this is in air, the air inside is moved when that outside is moved. For this reason the animal does not hear with every part of it, nor does the air penetrate everywhere; for it is not everywhere that the part which will be set in motion and made to sound has air. The air itself is soundless because it is easily dispersed; but when it is prevented from dispersing, its movement is sound. The air inside the ears has been walled up inside so as to be immovable, in order that it may accurately perceive all the varieties of movement. That is why we hear in water too, because the water does not penetrate into the very air which is naturally one with the ear; nor even into the ear, because of its convolutions. When this does happen, there is no hearing; nor is there if the tympanum membrane is injured, just as with the cornea of the eye [when it is injured]. Further, an indication of whether we hear or not is provided by whether there is always an echoing sound in the ear, as in a horn; for the air in the ears is always moving with a movement of its own. But sound is something external and not private to the ear. And that is why they say that we hear by means of what is empty and resonant, because we hear by means of that which has air confined within it.

420ª19. Is it the thing struck or the striker which makes the sound? Or is it indeed both, but in different ways? For sound is the movement of that which can be moved in the way in which things rebound from smooth surfaces when someone strikes them. Thus, not everything, as has been said, makes a noise when it is struck or striking something, e.g. if a needle strikes another; but the object struck must be of even surface, so that the air may rebound and vibrate as a mass.

420ª26. The differences between things which sound are revealed in the actual sound; for just as colours are not seen without light, so sharp and flat in pitch are not perceived without sound. These are so spoken of by transference from tangible objects; for that which is sharp moves the sense$_A$ to a great extent in a little time, while that which is flat moves it little in much time. Not that the sharp is quick and the flat slow, but the movement in the one case is such because of speed, in the other because of slowness. There seems to be an analogy with the sharp and blunt in the case of touch; for the sharp as it were stabs, while the blunt as it were thrusts, because the one produces motion in a short time, the other in a long, so that the one is incidentally quick, the other slow.

420ᵇ5. So much for our account of sound. Voice is a particular sound made by something with a soul; for nothing which does not have a soul has a voice, although such things may be said, by way of likeness, to have a voice, e.g. the pipe, lyre, and any other things which lack a soul but have variation in pitch, melody, and articulation; there is a likeness here because voice too has these properties. But many animals do not have a voice, e.g. those which are bloodless as well as fish among those which do have blood. And this is reasonable enough, since sound is a particular movement of air. But those fishes which are said to have a voice, e.g. ⟨those⟩ in the Achelous, make a sound

with their gills or some such part; but voice is sound made
by an animal and not with any chance part of its body.

420ᵇ14. But since everything which makes a sound does so
because something strikes something else in something
else again, and this last is air, it is reasonable that the only
creatures to have voice should be those which take in air.
For nature then uses the air breathed in for two functions;
just as it uses the tongue for both tasting and articulation,
and of these tasting is essential (and so is found in a greater
number of creatures), while expression is for the sake of
well-being, so also nature uses breath both to maintain the
inner warmth, as something essential (the reason will be
stated elsewhere), and also to produce voice so that there
may be well-being.

420ᵇ22. The organ of breathing is the throat, and that for
which this part exists is the lung; for it is through this part
that land animals have more warmth than other creatures.
It is also primarily the region round the heart which needs
breath. Hence the air must pass in when it is breathed in.

420ᵇ27. So, the striking of the inbreathed air upon what
is called the windpipe due to the soul in these parts constitutes voice. For, as we have said, not every sound made
by an animal is voice (for it is possible to make a sound
also with the tongue or as in coughing); but that which
does the striking must have a soul[1] and there must be a
certain imagination (for voice is a particular sound which
has meaning, and not one merely of the inbreathed air,
as a cough is; rather it is with this air that the animal
strikes the air in the windpipe against the windpipe itself).
An indication of this is the fact that we cannot use the

---

[1] Reading ἔμψυχόν with MSS. I have also removed the brackets round
the words 'for voice is a sound which has meaning'.

voice when breathing in or out, but only when holding the breath; for one who holds his breath produces the motion by its means. It is clear too why fish have no voice; for they have no throat. They do not have this part because they do not take in air or breathe in. The reason for this requires separate discussion$_L$.

CHAPTER 9

421ᵃ7. It is less easy to determine the nature of smell and the object of smell than that of the things already mentioned; for it is not so clear what sort of thing smell is as it is with sound or colour. The reason for this is that this sense$_A$ is, in our case, not accurate but is worse than with many animals; for man can smell things only poorly, and he perceives none of the objects of smell unless they are painful or pleasant, because the sense-organ is not accurate. It is reasonable to suppose that it is in this way too that hard-eyed animals perceive colours, and that the varieties of colour are not distinct for them, except in so far as they do or do not inspire fear. So too is the human race with regard to smells.

421ᵃ16. For it seems that smell has an analogy with taste, and the forms of flavour are in a similar position to those of smell, but in our case taste is more accurate because it is a form of touch, and it is this sense$_A$ which is most accurate in man; for in the others he is inferior to many animals, but in respect of touch he is accurate above all others. For this reason he is also the most intelligent of animals. An indication of this is the fact that in the human race natural ability and the lack of it depend on this sense-organ and on no other; for people with hard flesh are poorly endowed with thought, while those with soft flesh are well endowed.

421ª26. Just as flavours are sweet or bitter, so are smells. But some things have a corresponding smell and taste (I mean, for example, sweet smell and sweet taste) while other things have an opposite smell and taste. Similarly too a smell may be pungent, bitter, sharp, or oily. But, as we have said, because smells are not very distinct, as flavours are, they have taken their names from the latter in virtue of aresemblance in the things; for sweet {smell} belongs to saffron and honey and bitter to thyme and such like, and similarly in the other cases.

421ᵇ3. Smell is like hearing and each of the other senses_A, in that as hearing is of the audible and inaudible, and {sight} of the visible and invisible, so smell is of the odorous and inodorous. Some things are inodorous because it is impossible that they should have a smell at all,[1] others because they have a little and faint smell. The tasteless also is so spoken of similarly.

421ᵇ9. Smell too takes place through a medium, such as air or water; for water-animals too seem to perceive smell, whether they have or do not have blood, just as those which live in the air; for some of these, drawn by the smell, seek for their food from a great distance.

421ᵇ13. Hence there appears to be a problem, if all creatures have smell in the same way, yet man smells when inhaling but not when, instead of inhaling, he is exhaling or holding his breath, no matter whether the object is distant or near, or even if it is placed on the nostril. Also, that what is placed upon the sense-organ itself should be imperceptible is common to all animals,

[1] Reading παρὰ τὸ ὅλως ἀδύνατον ἔχειν ὀσμήν with most MSS.

but the inability to perceive without inhaling is peculiar to men; this is clear from experiment. So that the bloodless animals, since they do not inhale, would seem to have another sense$_A$ apart from those spoken of. But that is impossible, since they perceive smell; for, the perception$_A$ of the odorous, whether it be foul or fragrant, is smell. Moreover, they are evidently destroyed by the same strong odours as man is, e.g. bitumen, sulphur, and the like. They must, then, smell but without inhaling.

421^{b}26. It seems that in man this sense-organ differs from that of the other animals, just as his eyes differ from those of the hard-eyed animals—for his eyes have eyelids, as a screen and sheath, as it were, and he cannot see without moving or raising them. But the hard-eyed animals have nothing of this sort, but see straightaway what takes place in the transparent. In the same way, therefore, the sense-organ of smell$_K$ is in some creatures uncovered, like the eye, while in those which take in air it has a covering, which is removed when they inhale, owing to the dilatation of the veins and passages. And for this reason those animals which inhale do not smell in water; for in order to smell they must first inhale, and it is impossible to do this in water. Smell belongs to what is dry, just as flavour does to what is wet, and the sense-organ of smell$_K$ is potentially of such a kind.

CHAPTER 10

422^{a}8. The object of taste is a form of the tangible; and this is the reason why it is not perceptible through the medium of any foreign body; for no more is it so with touch. And the body in which the flavour resides, the object of taste, is in moisture as its matter; and this is a tangible thing. Hence even if we lived in water we should perceive a sweet object thrown into it; but the perception$_A$ would not have come to us through a medium but because of the mixture of the object with the moisture, just as in a drink. But colour is not seen in this way as the result of admixture, nor through effluences. There is nothing, then, here corresponding to a medium; but just as the object of sight is colour, so that of taste is flavour. Nothing produces the perception$_A$ of flavour without moisture, but it must have moisture actually or potentially, as is the case with salt; for it is easily dissolved and acts as a solvent on the tongue.

422ª20. Sight is of both the visible and the invisible (for darkness is invisible, and sight judges of this too), and further of that which is excessively bright (for this is invisible but in a different way from darkness). Similarly too hearing is of sound and silence, the one being audible, the other inaudible, and also of very loud sound as sight is of what is very bright (for just as a faint sound is inaudible so in a way is a loud and violent sound). And one thing is spoken of as invisible quite generally, like the impossible in other cases, while another is so spoken of if it is its nature to have the relevant quality but it fails to have it or has it imperfectly, parallel to the footless or kernel-less. So too taste is of the tasteable and the tasteless, the latter being that which has little or poor flavour or is destructive of taste. But the primary distinction seems to be between the drinkable and undrinkable (for both are a form of taste, but the latter is bad and destructive [of the sense of taste],[1] while the former is natural); and the drinkable is an object common to touch and taste.

---

[1] Reading γεῦσις γάρ τις ἀμφότερα· ἀλλὰ τὸ μὲν φαύλη καὶ φθαρτικὴ [τῆς γεύσεως], τὸ δὲ . . . with MSS. Ross's emendation is unnecessary.

422ᵃ34. Since the tasteable is moist, its sense-organ too must be neither actually moist nor incapable of being moistened. For taste is affected by the tasteable, *qua* tasteable. The sense-organ of taste, therefore, which is capable of being moistened while being preserved intact, but which is not itself moist, must be moistened. An indication of this is the fact that the tongue does not perceive either when it is very dry or when it is too wet; for in the latter case[1] there is a contact with the moisture which is there first, just as when someone first tastes a strong flavour and then tastes another, and as to sick people all things seem bitter because they perceive them with a tongue full of moisture of that kind.

422ᵇ10. The kinds of flavour, as in the case of colours, are, when simple, opposites: the sweet and the bitter; next to the one the oily and to the other the salt; and between these the pungent, the rough, the astringent, and the sharp. These seem to be just about all the varieties of flavour. Consequently, that which can taste$_K$ is potentially such, while that which makes it so actually is the object of taste.

CHAPTER 11

422ᵇ17. Concerning the tangible and touch the same account$_L$ may be given; for if touch is not one sense$_A$ but many, then the objects perceptible by touch must also be many. It is a problem whether it is many or one and also what is the sense-organ for that which can perceive by touch$_K$, whether it is the flesh and what is analogous to this in other creatures, or whether it is not, but the flesh is the medium, while the primary sense-organ is something

---

[1] Ross's emendation of ταύτῃ for αὕτη is dubious, but it makes little difference to the sense.

else which is internal. For every sense_A seems to be concerned with one pair of opposites, e.g. sight with white and black, hearing with high and low pitch, and taste with bitter and sweet; but in the object of touch there are many pairs of opposites, hot and cold, dry and wet, rough and smooth, and so on for the rest. There is *a* solution to this problem at any rate—that there are many pairs of opposites in the case of the other senses also, e.g. in vocal sound there is not only high and low pitch, but also loudness and softness, and smoothness and roughness of voice, and so on. There are other differences of this kind in the case of colour too. But what the one thing is which is the subject for touch as sound is for hearing is not clear.

422ᵇ34. Whether the sense-organ {for touch} is internal or whether it is not this but the flesh directly does not seem to receive an indication in the fact that perception_A occurs simultaneously with contact. For even as things are, if someone were to make a sort of membrane and stretch it round the flesh, it would communicate the sensation_A in the same way immediately when touched; and yet it is clear that the sense-organ would not be in this; and if this were to become naturally attached, the sensation_A would pass through it still more quickly. Hence, the part of the body which is of this kind seems to be to us as the air would be if it were naturally attached to us all round; for we should then have thought that we perceived sound, colour, and smell by virtue of a single thing, and that sight, hearing, and smell were a single sense_A. But as things are, because that through which the movements occur is separated from us, the sense-organs mentioned are manifestly different. But in the case of touch, this is, as things are, unclear; for the ensouled body cannot be composed of air or of water, for it must be something solid.

The remaining alternative is that it is a mixture of earth and these, as flesh and what is analogous to it tends to be; hence, the body must be the naturally adhering medium for that which can perceive by touch$_K$, and its perceptions$_A$ take place through it, manifold as they are. That they are manifold is made clear through touch in the case of the tongue; for it perceives all tangible objects with the same part as that with which it perceives flavour. If, then, the rest of the flesh perceived flavour, taste and touch would seem to be one and the same sense$_A$. But as things are they are two, because they are not interchangeable.

423ᵃ22. One might raise a problem here. Every body has depth, and that is the third dimension, and if between two bodies there exists a third it is not possible for them to touch each other. That which is moist or wet is not independent of body, but must be water or have water in it. Those things which touch each other in water must, since their extremities are not dry, have water between them, with which their extremities are full. If this is true, it is impossible for one thing to touch another in water, and similarly in air also (for air is related to things in it as water is to things in water, although we are more liable not to notice this, just as animals which live in water fail to notice whether the things which touch each other are wet). Does, then, the perception$_A$ of everything take place similarly, or is it different for different things, just as it is now thought that taste and touch act by contact, while the other senses act from a distance?

423ᵇ4. But this is not the case; rather we perceive the hard and the soft through other things also, just as we do that which can sound, the visible, and the odorous. But the latter are perceived from a distance, the former from close at hand, and for this reason the fact escapes our notice;

since we perceive all things surely through a medium, but in these cases we fail to notice. Yet, as we said earlier too, even if we perceived all objects of touch through a membrane without noticing that it separated us from them, we should be in the same position as we are now when in water or in air; for as things are we suppose that we touch the objects themselves and that nothing is through a medium.

423^b12. But there is a difference between the object of touch and those of sight and hearing, since we perceive them because the medium acts on us, while we perceive objects of touch not through the agency of the medium but simultaneously with the medium, like a man who is struck through his shield; for it is not that the shield is first struck and then strikes the man, but what happens is that both are struck simultaneously.

423^b17. It seems in general that just as air and water are to sight, hearing, and smell, so the flesh and the tongue are to their sense-organ as each of those is. And neither in the one case nor in the other would perception$_A$ occur when contact is made with the sense-organ itself, e.g. if someone were to put a white body on the surface of the eye. From this it is clear that that which can perceive$_K$ the object of touch is internal. For then the same thing would happen as in the other cases; for we do not perceive what is placed on the sense-organ, but we do perceive what is placed upon the flesh. Hence the flesh is the medium for that which can perceive by touch$_K$.

423^b27. It is the distinctive qualities of body, *qua* body, which are tangible. The qualities which I speak of as distinctive are those which determine the elements, hot and cold, dry and wet, of which we have spoken earlier in our account of the elements. Their sense-organ, that of touch$_K$, in which the sense$_A$ called touch primarily resides, is the part which is potentially such as they are. For perceiving is a form of being affected; hence, that which acts makes that part, which is potentially as it is, such as it is itself actually.

424^{a}2. For this reason we do not perceive anything which is equally as hot or cold, or hard or soft, but rather excesses of these, the sense$_A$ being a sort of mean between the opposites present in objects of perception. And that is why it judges objects of perception. For the mean is capable of judging; for it becomes to each extreme in turn the other extreme. And just as that which is to perceive white and black must be neither of them actually, although both potentially (and similarly too for the other senses), so in the case of touch that which is to perceive such must be neither hot nor cold.

424^{a}10. Again, just as sight was in a way of both the visible and the invisible, and just as the other senses too were similarly concerned with opposites, so too touch is of the tangible and the intangible; and the intangible is that which has to a very small degree the distinguishing characteristic of things which are tangible, as is the case with air, and also those tangible things which are in excess, as are those which are destructive. The situation with respect to each of the senses$_A$, then, has been stated in outline.

CHAPTER 12

424^{a}17. In general, with regard to all sense-perception$_A$, we must take it that the sense$_A$ is that which can receive perceptible forms without their matter, as wax receives the imprint of the ring without the iron or gold, and it takes the imprint which is of gold or bronze, but not *qua* gold or bronze. Similarly too in each case the sense$_A$ is affected by that which has colour or flavour or sound, but by these not in so far as they are what each of them is spoken of as being, but in so far as they are things of a certain kind and in accordance with their principle$_L$. The primary sense-organ is that in which such a potentiality resides. These are then the same, although what it is for them to be such is not the same. For that which perceives must be a particular extended magnitude, while what it is to be able to perceive and the sense$_A$ are surely not magnitudes, but rather a certain principle$_L$ and potentiality of that thing.

424ᵃ28. It is clear from all this too why excess in the objects of perception destroys the sense-organs (for if the movement is too violent for the sense-organ its principle$_L$ is destroyed—and this we saw the sense$_A$ to be—just as the consonance and pitch of the strings are destroyed when they are struck too violently). It is also clear why plants do not perceive, although they have a part of the soul and are affected by tangible objects; for they are cooled and warmed. The reason is that they do not have a mean, nor a first principle of a kind such as to receive the forms of objects of perception; rather they are affected by the matter as well.

424ᵇ3. Someone might raise the question whether that which cannot smell might be affected by smell, or that which cannot see by colour; and similarly in the other cases. If the object of smell is smell, then smell must produce, if anything, smelling; hence nothing which is unable to smell can be affected by smell (and the same account$_L$ applies to the other cases), nor can any of those things which can perceive be so affected except in so far as each is capable of perceiving. This is clear at the same time from the following too. Neither light and darkness nor sound nor smell does anything to bodies, but rather the things that they are in, e.g. it is the air accompanying the thunderbolt which splits the wood. But tangible objects and flavours do affect bodies; for otherwise by what could soulless things be affected and altered? Will those other objects, too, then, affect them? Or is it the case that not every body is affected by smell and sound, and those which are affected are indeterminate and inconstant, like air (for air smells, as if it had been affected)? What then is smelling apart from being affected? Or is smelling also perceiving, whereas the air when affected quickly becomes an object of perception?

BOOK III

CHAPTER 1

424^b22. That there is no other sense$_A$ apart from the five (and by these I mean sight, hearing, smell, taste, and touch) one might be convinced by the following considerations. We have even now perception$_A$ of everything of which touch is the sense$_A$ (for all the qualities of the tangible, *qua* tangible, are perceptible to us by touch). Also, if we lack any sense$_A$ we must also lack a sense-organ. Again, all the things which we perceive through direct contact are perceptible by touch, which we in fact have, while all those which we perceive through media and not by direct contact are perceptible by means of the elements (I mean, for example, air and water). And the situation is such that if two things different in kind from each other are perceptible through one thing, then whoever has a sense-organ of this kind must be capable of perceiving both (e.g. if the sense-organ is composed of air, and air is required both for sound and for colour); while if there is more than one medium for the same object, e.g. both air and water for colour (for both are transparent), then he who has one of these alone will perceive whatever is perceptible through both. Now, sense-organs are composed of two of these elements only, air and water (for the pupil of the eye is composed of water, the organ of hearing of air, and the organ of smell of one or other of these), while fire either belongs to none of them or is common to all (for nothing is capable of perceiving without warmth), and earth either belongs to none of them or is a constituent specially and above all of that of touch. So there would remain no sense-organ apart from those of water and air, and these some animals possess even now. It may be inferred then that all the senses$_A$ are possessed by those animals which are neither imperfect nor maimed (for even the mole apparently has eyes under the skin); hence, unless there is some other body and a property possessed by none of the bodies existing here and now, no sense$_A$ can be left out.

425ᵃ14. Nor again is it possible for there to be any special sense-organ for the common-objects, which we perceive by each sense$_A$ incidentally, e.g. movement, rest, figure, magnitude, number, and unity; for we perceive all these through movement, e.g. magnitude through movement (hence also figure, for figure is a particular form of magnitude), what is at rest through absence of movement, number through negation of continuity and also by the special-objects; for each sense$_A$ perceives one thing. Hence it is clear that it is impossible for there to be a special sense$_A$ for any of these, e.g. movement. For in that case it would be as we now perceive the sweet by sight; and this we do because we in fact have a perception$_A$ of both, as a result of which we recognize them at the same time when they fall together. (Otherwise we should perceive them in no other way than incidentally, as we perceive the son of Cleon not because he is the son of Cleon but because he is white, and the white object happens to be the son of Cleon). But for the common-objects we have even now a common sense$_A$, not incidentally; there is, then, no special {sense} for them; for if so we should not perceive them otherwise than as stated [that we see the son of Cleon].

425ᵃ30. The senses$_A$ perceive each other's special-objects incidentally, not in so far as they are themselves but in so far as they form a unity, when sense-perception$_A$ simultaneously takes place in respect of the same object, e.g. in respect of bile that it is bitter and yellow (for it is not the task of any further {perception} at any rate to say that both are one); hence too one may be deceived, and if something is yellow, one may think that it is bile.

425^{b}4. One might ask for what purpose we have several senses$_A$ and not one only. Is it perhaps in order that the common-objects which accompany {the special-objects}, e.g. movement, magnitude, and number, may be less likely to escape our notice? For if there were sight alone, and this was of white, they would be more likely to escape our notice and all things would seem to be the same because colour and magnitude invariably accompany each other. But as things are, since the common-objects are present in the objects of another sense too, this makes it clear that each of them is distinct.

CHAPTER 2

425^{b}12. Since we perceive that we see and hear, it must either be by sight that one perceives that one sees or by another {sense}. But in that case there will be the same {sense} for sight and the colour which is the subject for sight. So that either there will be two {senses} for the same thing or {the sense} itself will be the one for itself.

425^{b}15. Again, if the sense$_A$ concerned with sight were indeed different from sight, either there will be an infinite regress or there will be some {sense} which is concerned with itself; so that we had best admit this of the first in the series.

425^{b}17. But this presents a difficulty; for if to perceive by sight is to see, and if one sees colour or that which possesses

colour, then, if one is to see that which sees,[1] that which
sees[1] primarily will have colour. It is clear then that to
perceive by sight is not a single thing; for even when we do
not see, it is by sight that we judge both darkness and light,
though not in the same way. Moreover, [even that which
sees[1] is in a way coloured; for each sense-organ is receptive
of the object of perception without its matter. That is why
perceptions_A and imaginings remain in the sense-organs
even when the objects of perception are gone.]

*imprint
of the
image .*

425ᵇ26. The activity of the object of perception and of the
sense_A is one and the same, although what it is for them
to be such is not the same. I mean, for example, the actual
sound and the actual hearing; for it is possible to have
hearing and not to hear, and that which has sound is not
always sounding. But when that which can hear is active,
and that which can sound is sounding, then the actual hearing takes place at the same time as the actual sound, and
one might call these, the one listening, the other sounding.

426ª2. If then movement, i.e. acting [and being affected],
is in that which is acted upon, both the sound and hearing
as actual must be in that which is potentially hearing; for
the activity of that which can act and produce movement
takes place in that which is affected; for this reason it is
not necessary for that which produces movement to be
itself moved. The activity of that which can sound is sound
or sounding, while that of that which can hear_K is hearing
or listening; for hearing is twofold, and so is sound.

426ª8. The same account_L applies also to the other senses_A
and objects of perception. For just as both acting and being
affected are in that which is affected and not in that which
acts, so both the activity of the object of perception and

---

[1] Reading τὸ ὁρῶν with most MSS.

that of that which can perceive$_K$ are in that which can perceive$_K$. But in some cases they have a name, e.g. sounding and listening, while in others one or the other has no name; for, the activity of sight is spoken of as seeing, but that of colour has no name, while that of that which can taste$_K$ is tasting, but that of flavour has no name.

426ᵃ15. Since the activity of the object of perception and of that which can perceive$_K$ is one, though what it is for them to be such is not the same, the hearing and sound which are so spoken of must be simultaneously destroyed and simultaneously preserved, and so too for flavour and taste, and the rest similarly; but this is not necessary for those which are spoken of as potential. But the earlier philosophers of nature did not state the matter well, thinking that there is without sight nothing white nor black, nor flavour without tasting. For in one way they were right but in another wrong; for since perception$_A$ and the object of perception are so spoken of in two ways, as potential and as actual, the statement holds of the latter, but it does not hold of the former. But they spoke undiscriminatingly concerning things which are so spoken of *not* undiscriminatingly.

426ᵃ27. If voice is a kind of consonance, and voice and hearing are in a way one [and the same thing is in a way not one], and if consonance is a proportion$_L$, then hearing must also be a kind of proportion$_L$. And it is for this reason too that either excess, whether high or low pitch, destroys hearing; and in the same way in flavours excess destroys taste, and in colours the too bright or dark destroys sight, and so too in smelling with strong smell, whether sweet or bitter, since the sense$_A$ is a kind of proportion$_L$. For this reason too things are pleasant when brought pure and

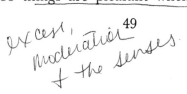

excess, moderation
⁴⁹
of the senses.

unmixed to the proportion$_L$, e.g. the high-pitched, sweet or salt, for they are pleasant then; but in general a mixture, a consonance, is more pleasant than either high or low pitch, [and for taste the more pleasant is that which is capable of being further warmed or cooled]. The sense$_A$ is a proportion$_L$; and objects in excess dissolve or destroy it.

426ᵇ8 Each sense$_A$, therefore, is concerned with the subject perceived by it, being present in the sense-organ, *qua* sense-organ, and it judges the varieties of the subject perceived by it, e.g. sight for white and black, and taste for sweet and bitter; and similarly for the other senses too. Since we judge both white and sweet and each of the objects of perception by reference to each other, by what do we perceive also that they differ? This must indeed be by perception$_A$; for they are objects of perception. From this it is clear also that flesh is not the ultimate sense-organ; for if it were it would be necessary for that which judges to judge when it is itself touched.

426ᵇ17. Nor indeed is it possible to judge by separate means that sweet is different from white, but both must be evident to one thing—for otherwise, even if I perceived one thing and you another, it would be evident that they were different from each other. Rather one thing must assert that they are different; for sweet is different from white. The same thing then asserts this; hence, as it asserts so it both thinks and perceives. That, therefore, it is not possible to judge separate things by separate means is clear.

426ᵇ23. And that it is not possible either at separate times is clear from the following. For just as it is the same thing which asserts that good and bad are different, so also when it asserts that the one and the other are different the time when is not incidental (I mean as, for example, when I say now that they are different, but not that they are different now); but it so asserts both now and that they are different now; all at the same time, therefore. Hence, it is undivided and does this in an undivided time.

426ᵇ29. But yet it is impossible for the same thing to be moved simultaneously with opposite motions, in so far as it is indivisible, and in an indivisible time. For if something is sweet it moves perception$_A$ or thought in one way, while the bitter moves it in the opposed way, while white moves it quite differently. Is, then, that which judges at the same time both numerically indivisible and undivided, while divided in what it is for it to be such? It is indeed in one way that which is divided which perceives divided objects, but in another way it is this *qua* indivisible; for in what it is for it to be such it is divided, while it is indivisible in place and number. Or is this impossible? For the same indivisible thing may be both opposites potentially, although it is not so in what it is for it to be such, but it becomes divided when actualized; and it is not possible for it to be simultaneously white and black, so that it cannot also be affected simultaneously by forms of these, if perception$_A$ and thought are of this kind.

427ᵃ9. But it is like what some call a point, which is ⟨both indivisible⟩ and divisible in so far as it is one and two. That which judges, therefore, is one and judges at one time in so far as it is indivisible, but in so far as it is divisible it simultaneously uses the same point twice. In so far then as it uses the boundary-point twice it judges two separate things[1] in a way separately; in so far as it uses it as one it judges one thing and at one time.

---

[1] Retaining κεχωρισμένα.

427ᵃ14. So much then by way of discussion about the first principle in virtue of which we say that an animal is capable of perceiving.

CHAPTER 3

427ᵃ17. There are two distinguishing characteristics by which people mainly define the soul: motion in respect of place; and thinking, understanding, and perceiving. Thinking and understanding are thought to be like a form of perceiving (for in both of these the soul judges and recognizes some existing thing). Indeed the ancients say that understanding and perceiving are the same. Empedocles for instance said 'Wisdom increases for men according to what is present to them' and elsewhere 'Whence different thoughts continually present themselves to them'. And Homer's 'Such is the mind of men' means the same thing too. For all these take thinking to be corporeal, like perceiving, and both perceiving and understanding to be of like by like, as we explained in our initial discussion_L. (Yet they should at the same time have said something about error, for this is more characteristic of animals and the soul spends more time in this state; hence on their view either all appearances must be true, as some say, or error must be a contact with the unlike, for this is the opposite of recognizing like by like. But error and knowledge seem to be the same in respect of the opposites.) That perceiving and understanding, therefore, are not the same is clear. For all animals have the former, but few the latter. Nor again is thinking, in which one can be right and wrong, right thinking being understanding, knowledge, and true belief, wrong the opposite of these—nor is this the same as perceiving. For the perception_A of the special-objects is always true and is found in all animals, whereas it is possible to think falsely also, and thinking is found in no animal in which there is not also reason$_L$; for imagination is different from both perception$_A$ and thought, and this does not occur without perception$_A$, nor supposal without it.

427ᵇ16. That imagination is not the same kind of thinking[1] as supposal is clear. For the former is up to us when we wish (for it is possible to produce something before our eyes, as those do who set things out in mnemonic systems and form images of them); but believing is not up to us, for it must be either true or false. Moreover, when we believe that something is terrible or alarming we are immediately affected correspondingly, and similarly if it is something encouraging; but in the case of the imagination we are just as if we saw the terrible or encouraging things in a picture.

427ᵇ24. There are also varieties of supposal itself, knowledge, belief, understanding, and their opposites, but the difference between these must be left for another discussion$_L$.

427ᵇ27. As for thought, since it is different from perceiving and seems to include on the one hand imagination and on the other supposal, we must determine about imagination before going on to discuss the other. Now if imagination is that in virtue of which we say that an image occurs to us and not as we speak of it metaphorically, is it one of those potentialities or dispositions in virtue of which we judge and are correct or incorrect? Such are perception$_A$, belief, knowledge, and intellect.

428ª5 Now, that it is not perception$_A$ is clear from the following. Perception$_A$ is either a potentiality like sight or

---

[1] Retaining νόησις.

53

imag. has ethical value?

perception
v.
imagination

an activity like seeing; but something can appear to us when neither of these is present, e.g. things in dreams. Secondly, perception is always present but not imagination. But if they were the same in actuality it would be possible for all beasts to have imagination; and it seems that this is not so, e.g. the ant or bee, and the grub.[1] Next, {perceptions} are always true, while imaginings are for the most part false. Further, it is not when we are exercising {our senses} accurately with regard to objects of perception that we say that this appears to us to be a man, but rather when we do not perceive it distinctly; and then it may be either true or false.[2] And, as we said before, sights appear to us even with the eyes closed.

428ᵃ16. Nor again will imagination be any of those things which are always correct, e.g. knowledge or intellect; for imagination can be false also. It remains, then, to see if it is belief; for belief may be either true or false. But conviction follows on belief (for it is not possible to believe things without being convinced of them); and while no beast has conviction, many have imagination. Furthermore every belief implies conviction, conviction implies being persuaded, and persuasion implies reason_L; some beasts have imagination, but none reason_L.[3]

428ᵃ24. It is clear, therefore, that imagination will be neither belief together with perception_A, nor belief through perception_A, nor a blend of belief and percep-

---

[1] The MS. reading is puzzling since it is doubtful whether Aristotle would have denied imagination to ants and bees. Förster's (and O.C.T.'s) emendation καὶ σκώληκι for ἢ σκώληκι does not really achieve anything. It is possibly right to accept Torstrik's emendation μύρμηκι μὲν ἢ μελίττῃ, σκώληκι δ' οὔ, to be translated 'ants and bees do, but the grub does not'.

[2] Reading τότε ἢ ἀληθὴς and not Ross's emendation πότερον ἀληθὴς.

[3] Retaining the MS. text without brackets suggesting deletion.

tion$_A$, both on these grounds and because it is clear that[1] on that view the belief will have as object nothing else but that which, if it exists, is the object of the perception too. I mean that it will be the blend of the belief in white and the perception$_A$ of white that will be imagination; for it will surely not come about from the belief in the good and the perception$_A$ of white. Something's appearing to us will then be believing what one perceives and not incidentally. But things can also appear falsely, when we have at the same time a true supposition about them, e.g. the sun appears a foot across, although we believe it to be bigger than the inhabited world. So it follows on this view either that we shall have abandoned the true belief that we had, although the circumstances remain as they were, and we have not forgotten it or been persuaded to the contrary, or, if we still have it, the same one must be both true and false. But it could become false only if the circumstances changed without our noticing. Imagination, then, is not any one of these things nor is it formed from them.

428ᵇ10. But since it is possible when one thing is moved for another to be moved by it, and since imagination is thought to be a kind of movement and not to occur apart from sense-perception$_A$ but only in things which perceive and with respect to those things of which there is perception$_A$, since too it is possible for movement to occur as the result of the activity of perception$_A$, and this must be like the perception$_A$—this movement cannot exist apart from sense-perception$_A$ or in things which do not perceive; and in respect of it, it is possible for its possessor to do and be affected by many things, and it may be both true and false.

---

[1] Reading δῆλον ὅτι with MSS. or possibly ὅτι δῆλον ὅτι with Shorey.

428ᵇ17. This happens for the following reasons: Perception$_A$ of the special-objects is true or is liable to falsity to the least possible extent. Secondly {there is the perception} that those things which are incidental to these objects of perception are so; and here now it is possible to be in error, for we are not mistaken on the point that there is white, but about whether the white object is this thing or another we may be mistaken. Thirdly {there is perception} of the common-objects which follow upon the incidental-objects to which the special-objects belong (I mean, for example, movement and magnitude);[1] and about these then it is most possible to be in error in sense-perception$_A$.

428ᵇ25. The movement which comes about as a result of the activity of sense-perception$_A$ will differ in so far as it comes from these three kinds of perception$_A$. The first is true as long as perception$_A$ is present, while the others may be false whether it is present or absent, and especially when the object of perception is far off.

428ᵇ30. If, then, nothing else has the stated characteristics except imagination, and this is what was said, imagination will be a movement taking place as a result of actual sense-perception$_A$. And since sight is sense-perception$_A$ *par excellence*, the name for imagination (*phantasia*) is taken from light (*phaos*), because without light it is not possible to see. And because imaginations persist and are similar to perceptions$_A$, animals do many things in accordance with them, some because they lack reason, viz. beasts, and others because their reason is sometimes obscured by passion, disease, or sleep, viz. men. As to what imagination is, then, and why, let this suffice.

---

[1] Accepting Bywater's transposition of the words ἃ συμβέβηκε τοῖς αἰσθητοῖς to line 20, as in the O.C.T.

CHAPTER 4

429ᵃ10. In respect of that part of the soul by which the soul both knows and understands, whether this is distinct or not distinct spatially but only in definition$_L$, we must inquire what distinguishing characteristic it has, and how thinking ever comes about.

429ᵃ13. Now, if thinking is akin to perceiving, it would be either being affected in some way by the object of thought or something else of this kind. It must then be unaffected, but capable of receiving the form, and potentially such as it, although not identical with it; and as that which is capable of perceiving$_K$ is to the objects of perception, so must be the intellect similarly to its objects.

429ᵃ18. It must, then, since it thinks all things, be un-mixed, as Anaxagoras says, in order that it may rule, that is in order that it may know; for the intrusion of anything foreign to it hinders and obstructs it; hence too, it must have no other nature than this, that it is potential. That part of the soul, then, called intellect (and I speak of as intellect that by which the soul thinks and supposes) is actually none of existing things before it thinks. Hence too, it is reasonable that it should not be mixed with the body; for in that case it would come to be of a certain kind, either cold or hot, or it would even have an organ like the faculty of perception$_K$; but as things are it has none. Those who say, then, that the soul is a place of forms speak well, except that it is not the whole soul but that which can think, and it is not actually but potentially the forms.

429ᵃ29. That the ways in which the faculties of sense-perception$_K$ and intellect$_K$ are unaffected are not the

57

same is clear from reference to the sense-organs and the sense$_A$. For the sense$_A$ is not capable of perceiving when the object of perception has been too intense, e.g. it cannot perceive sound after loud sounds, nor see or smell after strong colours or smells. But when the intellect thinks something especially fit for thought, it thinks inferior things not less but rather more. For the faculty of sense-perception$_K$ is not independent of the body, whereas the intellect is distinct. When the intellect has become each thing in the way that one who actually knows is said to do so (and this happens when he can exercise his capacity by himself), it exists potentially even then in a way, although not in the same way as before it learned or discovered; and then it can think by itself.

429^{b}10. Since a magnitude and what it is to be a magnitude are different, and water and what it is to be water (and so too for many other things, but not for all; for in some cases they are the same), we judge what it is to be flesh and flesh itself either by means of something different or by the same thing differently disposed. For flesh does not exist apart from matter, but like the snub it is a this in a this. It is, then, with the faculty of sense-perception$_K$ that we judge the hot and the cold and those things of which flesh is a certain proportion$_L$. But it is by something else, either something distinct or something which is to the former as a bent line is related to itself when straightened out, that we judge what it is to be flesh.

429^{b}18. Again, in the case of those things which exist in abstraction, the straight corresponds to the snub, for it involves extension; but 'what it is for it to be what it was', if what it is to be straight and the straight are different, is something else; let it be duality. We judge it, then, by something different or by the same thing differently disposed. In general, then, as things are distinct from matter, so it is too with what concerns the intellect.

429^{b}22. Given that the intellect is something simple and unaffected, and that it has nothing in common with anything else, as Anaxagoras says, someone might raise these questions: how will it think, if thinking is being affected in some way (for it is in so far as two things have something in common that the one is thought to act and the other to be affected)? And can it itself also be thought? For either everything else will have intellect, if it can itself be thought without this being through anything else and if what can be thought is identical in form, or it will have something mixed in it which makes it capable of being thought as the other things are.

429^{b}29. Now, being affected in virtue of something common has been discussed before—to the effect that the intellect is in a way potentially the objects of thought, although it is actually nothing before it thinks; potentially in the same way as there is writing on a tablet on which nothing actually written exists; that is what happens in the case of the intellect. And it is itself an object of thought, just as its objects are. For, in the case of those things which have no matter, that which thinks and that which is thought are the same; for contemplative knowledge and that which is known in that way are the same. The reason why it does not always think we must consider. In those things which have matter each of the objects of thought is present potentially. Hence, *they* will not have intellect in them (for intellect is a potentiality for being such things without their matter), while *it* will have what can be thought in it.

CHAPTER 5

430ª10. Since [just as] in the whole of nature there is
something which is matter to each kind of thing (and this
is what is potentially all of them), while on the other hand
there is something else which is their cause and is pro-
ductive by producing them all—these being related as an
art to its material—so there must also be these differences
in the soul. And there is an intellect which is of this kind
by becoming all things, and there is another which is so
by producing all things, as a kind of disposition, like light,
does; for in a way light too makes colours which are
potential into actual colours. And this intellect is distinct,
unaffected, and unmixed, being in essence activity.

430ª18. For that which acts is always superior to that which
is affected, and the first principle to the matter. [Actual
knowledge is identical with its object; but potential knowledge is prior in time in the individual but not prior even
in time in general]; and it is not the case that it sometimes
thinks and at other times not.[1] In separation it is just what
it is, and this alone is immortal and eternal. (But we do not
remember because this is unaffected, whereas the passive
intellect is perishable, and without this thinks nothing.)[2]

CHAPTER 6

430ª26. The thinking of undivided objects is among those
things about which there is no falsity. Where there is both
falsity and truth, there is already a combination of
thoughts as forming a unity—as Empedocles said 'where
in many cases heads grew without necks' and were then

[1] The brackets are mine. The sentence is repeated at 431ª1, and has
probably been substituted here for a reference to the active intellect, which
is required for what follows.   [2] Bracketing different from O.C.T.

joined together by Love—so too these things, previously separate, are combined, e.g. the incommensurable and the diagonal; and if the thinking is concerned with things that have been or will be, then time is thought of in addition and combined in the thought. For falsity always depends upon a combination; for even if someone says that white is non-white he combines ⟨white and⟩ non-white.[1] It is possible to say that these are all divisions too. But at any rate, it is not only that Cleon is white that is false or true but also that he was or will be. And that which produces a unity is in each case the intellect.

430ᵇ6. Since the undivided is twofold, either potentially or actually, nothing prevents one thinking of the undivided when one thinks of a length (for this is actually undivided), and that in an undivided time; for the time is divided and undivided in a similar way to the length. It is not possible to say what one was thinking of in each half time; for these do not exist, except potentially, if the whole is not divided. But if one thinks of each of the halves separately, then one divides the time also simultaneously; and then it is as if they were lengths themselves. But if one thinks of the whole as made up of both halves, then one does so in the time made up of both halves.

430ᵇ16. That which is thought and the time in which it is thought are divided incidentally and not as those things were, although they are undivided as they were; for there is in these too something undivided, although surely not separate, which makes the time and the length unities. And this exists similarly in everything which is continuous, both time and length.

[1] Reading the text with Ross's addition of the words φῇ, τὸ λευκὸν καί, though the addition is perhaps scarcely necessary, even if 'says' has to be supplied.

430ᵇ14. That which is undivided not quantitatively but in form one thinks of in an undivided time and with an undivided part of the soul.¹

430ᵇ20. The point and every division, and that which is in this way undivided, are made known as privation is. And the same account_L applies to the other cases, e.g. how one recognizes evil or black; for one recognizes them in a way by their opposites. That which recognizes must be its object potentially, †and the latter must be in it.†² But if there is anything, †some one of the causes,†² which has no opposite, then this will know itself and is activity and distinct.

430ᵇ26. Every assertion says something of something, as too does denial, and is true or false. But not every thought is such; that of what a thing is in respect of 'what it is for it to be what it was' is true, and does not say something of something. But just as the seeing of a special-object³ is true, while the seeing whether the white thing is a man or not is not always true, so it is with those things which are without matter.

CHAPTER 7

431ª1. Actual knowledge is identical with its object. But potential knowledge is prior in time in the individual, but not prior even in time in general; for all things that come to be are derived from that which is so actually.

---

¹ Accepting Bywater's transposition of this sentence.
² The O.C.T. includes these words in daggers, suggesting that the text is corrupt; but the text could stand in the first of the two cases, although its interpretation demands a change of subject.
³ Ross daggers the words τοῦ ἰδίου and suggests tentatively in addition that the words τι λευκὸν might be substituted. This is unnecessary.

431ª4. It is clear that the object of perception makes that which can perceive$_K$ actively so instead of potentially so; for it is not affected or altered. Hence this is a different form from movement; for movement is an activity of the incomplete, while activity proper is different, the activity of the complete.

431ª8. Perceiving, then, is like mere assertion and thought; when something is pleasant or painful, {the soul} pursues or avoids it, as it were asserting or denying it; and to feel pleasure or pain is to be active with the perceptive mean towards the good or bad as such. Avoidance and desire, as actual, are the same thing, and that which can desire$_K$ and that which can avoid$_K$ are not different either from each other or from that which can perceive$_K$; but what it is for them to be such is different. To the thinking soul images serve as sense-perceptions (*aisthēmata*). And when it asserts or denies good or bad, it avoids or pursues it. Hence the soul never thinks without an image.

431ª17. And just as the air makes the pupil such and such, and this in turn something else, and the organ of hearing likewise, and the last thing in the series is one thing, and a single mean, although what it is for it to be such is plural . . .

431ª20. What it is by which one determines the difference between sweet and hot has been stated already, but we must say also the following. It is one thing, but it is so as a boundary is, and these things, being one by analogy and number, are ⟨each⟩ to each as those are to each other; for what difference does it make to ask how one judges those things which are not of the same kind or those which are opposites, like white and black? Now let it be the case that as *A*, white, is to *B*, black, so *C* is to *D* [as those are to each

63

other]; so that it holds *alternando* too. Now if CD[1] were to belong to one thing, then it would be the case, as for AB too, that they would be one and the same, although what it is for them to be such is not the same—and similarly for those others. And the same account$_L$ would apply if A were sweet and B white.

431ᵇ2. That which can think$_K$, therefore, thinks the forms in images, and just as in those what is to be pursued and avoided is determined for it, so, apart from sense-perception$_A$, when it is concerned with images, it is moved, e.g. perceiving that the beacon is alight you recognize[2] when you see it moving that it belongs to the enemy, but sometimes you calculate on the basis of images or thoughts in the soul, as if seeing, and plan what is going to happen in relation to present affairs. And when one says, as there, that something is pleasant or painful, so here one avoids or pursues—and so in action[3] generally. That which is apart from action too, the true and the false, are in the same genus as the good and bad; but they differ, the first being absolute, the second relative to someone.

431ᵇ12. Those things which are spoken of as in abstraction one thinks of just as, if one thought actually of the snub, not *qua* snub, but separately *qua* hollow, one would think of it apart from the flesh in which the hollow exists[4]— one thinks of mathematical entities which are not separate, as separate, when one thinks of them.[5]

---

[1] Reading 'CD ... AB' with MSS., rather than 'CA ... DB' with O.C.T.

[2] Deleting τῇ κοινῇ with Bywater.   [3] Reading ἐν πράξει with MSS.

[4] Taking the text as emended in O.C.T. But the traditional text could be given a plausible interpretation—'just as one might think of the snub; *qua* snub one would not think of it separately but *qua* hollow, if anyone actually thought of it, one would think of it apart from the flesh, etc.'

[5] Deleting the ἤ added by the O.C.T. before ἐκεῖνα, as unnecessary and perhaps misleading. The addition of ὄντα after οὐ κεχωρισμένα is also unnecessary.

431ᵇ17. In general, the intellect in activity is its objects. Whether or not it is possible for the intellect to think of any objects which are separate from spatial magnitude when it is itself not so separate must be considered later.

CHAPTER 8

431ᵇ20. Now, summing up what has been said about the soul, let us say again that the soul is in a way all existing things; for existing things are either objects of perception or objects of thought, and knowledge is in a way the objects of knowledge and perception$_4$ the objects of perception. How this is so we must inquire.

431ᵇ24. Knowledge and perception$_4$ are divided to correspond to their objects, the potential to the potential, the actual to the actual. In the soul that which can perceive$_K$ and that which can know$_K$ are potentially these things, the one the object of knowledge, the other the object of perception. These must be either the things themselves or their forms. Not the things themselves; for it is not the stone which is in the soul, but its form. Hence the soul is as the hand is; for the hand is a tool of tools, and the intellect is a form of forms and sense$_4$ a form of objects of perception.

432ᵃ3. Since there is no actual thing which has separate existence, apart from, as it seems, magnitudes which are objects of perception, the objects of thought are included among the forms which are objects of perception, both those that are spoken of as in abstraction and those which are dispositions and affections of objects of perception. And for this reason unless one perceived things one would not learn or understand anything, and when one contemplates one must simultaneously contemplate an image;

knowledge not of things but of their appearances —

for images are like sense-perceptions (aisthēmata), except that they are without matter. But imagination is different from assertion and denial; for truth and falsity involve a combination of thoughts. But what distinguishes the first thoughts from images? Surely neither these nor any other thoughts will be images, but they will not exist without images.

CHAPTER 9

432ª15. The soul of animals has been defined by reference to two potentialities, that concerned with judgement$_K$, which is the function of thought and sense-perception$_A$, and secondly that for producing movement in respect of place. Let so much suffice about perception$_A$ and the intellect; we must now inquire what it is in the soul which produces movement, whether it is one part of it separate either spatially or in definition$_L$, or whether it is the whole soul, and if it is one part, whether it is a special part in addition to those usually spoken of and those which we have mentioned, or whether it is one of these.

432ª22. A problem arises straightaway, in what way we should speak of parts of the soul and how many there are. For in one way there seem to be an indefinite number and not only those which some mention in distinguishing them—the parts concerned with reasoning$_K$, passion$_K$, and wanting$_K$, or according to others the rational and irrational parts; for in virtue of the distinguishing characteristics by which they distinguish these parts, there will clearly be other parts too with a greater disparity between them than these, those which we have already discussed, the nutritive$_K$, which belongs both to plants and to all animals, and the perceptive$_K$, which could not easily be set down as either irrational or rational. There is again the part concerned with the imagination$_K$, which is different from all of them in what it is for it to be such, although with which of them it is identical or non-identical presents a great problem, if we are to posit separate parts of the soul. In addition to these there is the part concerned with desire$_K$, which would seem to be different from all both in definition$_L$ and in potentiality. And it would be absurd surely to split this up; for in the part concerned with reasoning$_K$ there will be wishing, and in the irrational part wanting and passion; and if the soul is tripartite there will be desire in each part.

432ᵇ7. To come then to the point with which our discussion$_L$ is now concerned, what is it that moves the animal in respect of place? For, movement in respect of growth and decay, which all have, would seem to be produced by what all have, the faculties of generation$_K$ and nutrition$_K$. We must inquire also later concerning breathing in and out, and sleep and waking; for these too present great difficulty.

432ᵇ13. But as for movement in respect of place, we must inquire what it is that produces in the animal the movement involved in travelling. That, then, it is not the nutritive potentiality is clear; for this movement is always for the sake of something and involves imagination and desire; for nothing which is not desiring or avoiding something moves unless as the result of force. Besides, plants would then be capable of movement and they would have some part instrumental for this kind of movement.

432ᵇ19. Similarly it is not the faculty of sense-perception$_K$ either; for there are many animals which have sense-perception$_A$ but are stationary and unmoving throughout.

If, then, nature does nothing without reason and never fails in anything that is necessary, except in creatures which are maimed or imperfect, while the animals of this kind are perfect and not maimed (an indication being that they can reproduce themselves and have a maturity and a decline)—then it follows too that they would have parts instrumental for travelling.

432b26. Nor is it the part concerned with reasoning$_K$ and what is called the intellect that produces the movement; for the contemplative intellect contemplates nothing practicable, and says nothing about what is to be avoided and pursued, while the movement always belongs to one who is avoiding or pursuing something. But even when it contemplates something of the kind, it does not straight away command avoidance or pursuit, e.g. it often thinks of something fearful or pleasant, but it does not command fear, although the heart is moved, or, if the object is pleasant, some other part.

433a1. Again, even if the intellect enjoins us and thought tells us to avoid or pursue something, we are not moved, but we act in accordance with our wants, as the incontinent man does. And in general we see that the man who has the art of healing does not always heal, this implying that there is something else which is responsible for action in accordance with knowledge and not knowledge itself. Nor is desire responsible for this movement; for continent people, even when they desire and want things, do not do those things for which they have the desire, but they follow reason.

CHAPTER 10

433ª9. It is at any rate clear that these two produce movement, either desire or intellect, if we set down the imagination as a kind of thought; for many follow their imaginations against their knowledge, and in the other animals thought and reasoning do not exist, although imagination does. Both of these, therefore, can produce movement in respect of place, intellect and desire, but intellect which reasons for the sake of something and is practical; and it differs from the contemplative intellect in respect of the end. Every desire too is for the sake of something; for the object of desire is the starting-point for the practical intellect, and the final step is the starting-point for action.

433ª17. Hence it is reasonable that these two appear the sources of movement, desire and practical thought. For the object of desire produces movement, and, because of this, thought produces movement, because the object of desire is its starting-point. And when the imagination produces movement it does not do so without desire. Thus there is one thing which produces movement, the faculty of desire$_K$. For if there were two things which produced movement, intellect and desire, they would do so in virtue of some common form; but as things are, the intellect does not appear to produce movement without desire (for wishing is a form of desire, and when one is moved in accordance with reasoning, one is moved in accordance with one's wish too), and desire produces movement even contrary to reasoning; for wanting is a form of desire.

433ª26. Intellect then is always right; but desire and imagination are both right and not right. Hence it is always the object of desire which produces movement, but this is either the good or the apparent good; not every good but the practicable good. And it is that which can also be otherwise that is practicable.

433ª31. That therefore it is a potentiality of the soul of this kind, that which is called desire, that produces movement is clear. But for those who divide the soul into parts, if they divide and distinguish them according to potentialities, it transpires that there are many parts, the nutritive$_K$, perceptive$_K$, thinking$_K$, deliberative$_K$, and furthermore that concerned with desire$_K$; for these differ more from each other than do the parts concerned with wanting$_K$ and passion$_K$.

433ᵇ5. But desires arise which are opposed to each other, and this happens when reason$_L$ and wants are opposed and it takes place in creatures which have a perception$_A$ of time (for the intellect bids us resist on account of the future, while our wants bid us act on account of what is immediate; for what is immediately pleasant seems both absolutely pleasant and absolutely good because we do not see the future). Hence that which produces movement will be one in kind, the faculty of desire$_K$ as such—and first of all the object of desire (for this produces movement without being moved, by being thought of or imagined)—though numerically there will be more than one thing which produces movement.

433ᵇ13. There are three things, one that which produces movement, second that whereby it does so, and third again that which is moved, and that which produces movement is twofold, that which is unmoved and that which produces movement and is moved. That which is unmoved is the practical good, and that which produces movement and is moved is the faculty of desire$_K$ (for that which is moved is moved in so far as it desires, and desire as actual is a form of movement), while that which is moved is the animal; and the instrument by which desire produces movement is then something bodily. Hence it must be investigated among the functions common to body and soul.

433ᵇ21. To speak in summary fashion for the present—that which produces movement instrumentally is found where a beginning and an end are the same, e.g. in the hinge-joint; for there the convex and the concave are respectively the end and the beginning of movement (hence the latter is at rest but the former moves), the two being different in definition$_L$, but spatially inseparable. For everything is moved by pushing and pulling; hence, as in a circle, one point must remain fixed and the movement must begin from this. In general, therefore, as we have said, in so far as the animal is capable of desire so far is it capable of moving itself; and it is not capable of desire without imagination. And all imagination is either concerned with reasoning or perception. In the latter then the other animals share also.

CHAPTER 11

433ᵇ31. We must consider also what it is that produces movement in the imperfect animals which have perception$_A$ by touch only—whether they can have imagination and wants, or not. For they evidently have pain and pleasure, and if these they must have wants also. But how could they have imagination? Or is it that just as they are moved indeterminately, so also they have these things, but indeterminately?

434ᵃ5. Imagination concerned with perception, as we have

said, is found in the other animals also, but that concerned
with deliberation in those which are capable of reasoning
(for the decision whether to do this or that is already a
task for reasoning; and one must measure by a single
standard; for one pursues what is superior; hence one has
the ability to make one image out of many).

434ᵃ10. The reason why these animals are thought not
to have beliefs is that they do not have beliefs derived
from inference [but this has that]. Hence desire does not
imply the deliberative faculty. Sometimes it overcomes
and moves a wish; sometimes the latter does this to the
former, like a ball, one desire overcoming the other, when
incontinence occurs.[1] But by nature the higher is always
predominant and effective; so that three motions are
thereby involved. But the faculty of knowledge$_K$ is not
moved but remains constant.

434ᵃ16. Since the one supposition and proposition$_L$ is
universal and the other is particular (the one saying that
such and such a man ought to do such and such a thing,
while the other says that this then is such and such a thing,
and I am such and such a man), then either it is the latter
opinion, not the universal one, which produces movement,
or it is both, but the first is more static while the other is not.

CHAPTER 12

434ᵃ22. Everything then that lives and has a soul must
have the nutritive soul, from birth until death; for anything that has been born must have growth, maturity, and
decline, and these things are impossible without nourish-

---

[1] Retaining the MSS. reading: νικᾷ δ' ἐνίοτε τὴν βούλησιν· ὁτὲ δ' ἐκείνη
ταύτην, ὥσπερ σφαῖρα, ἡ ὄρεξις . . . .

ment. The potentiality for nutrition must then be present in all things which grow and decline.

434^{a}27. Sense-perception$_A$ is not necessary in all living things; for those things which have a body which is simple cannot have touch [and without this nothing can be an animal], nor can those which cannot receive forms without the matter. Animals must have sense-perception$_A$ ⟨and without this nothing can be an animal⟩, if nature does nothing without reason. For everything in nature exists for the sake of something or will be an accident of those things which are for the sake of something. Grant then that every body which can travel would, if it did not have sense-perception$_A$, perish and fail to reach its end, which is the function of nature. (For how would it be nourished? For stationary creatures get this from the source from which they have been born, but if it is not stationary but is generated, a body cannot have a soul and an intellect capable of judgement and not have sense-perception$_A$, [nor if it is ungenerated],[1] for why would it have it?[2] For this would have to be to the advantage of either the soul or the body, but in fact it would be neither; for the soul would not think any better and the body would be no better because of that.) No body, therefore, which is not stationary has a soul without sense-perception$_A$.

434^{b}9. Further, if it does have sense-perception$_A$, the body must be either simple or composite. But it cannot be simple; for then it would not have touch, and it must have this. This is clear from the following. Since the animal is an ensouled body, and every body is tangible, and it is that which is perceptible by touch which is tangible, the body of an animal must also be capable of touch, if the

---

[1] The words ἀλλὰ μὴν οὐδὲ ἀγένητον should probably be deleted; they interrupt the thread of the argument.   [2] Deleting the οὐχ.

animal is to survive. For the other senses$_A$, smell, sight, and hearing, perceive through other things, but anything which touches things will be unable, if it does not have sense-perception$_A$, to avoid some of them and take others. If that is so, it will be impossible for the animal to survive.

434^{b}18. For that reason, taste too is a form of touch; for it is concerned with food, and food is a tangible body. Sound, colour, and smell do not nourish, nor do they produce either growth or decay; so that taste too must be a form of touch, because it is a perception$_A$ of what is tangible and nourishing. These {senses}, therefore, are necessary to the animal, and it is clear that it is not possible for an animal to exist without touch. But the others are necessary for the sake of well-being and not for every kind of animal no matter what, although they must exist in some, e.g. those capable of travelling. For if they are to survive, they must perceive not only when in contact with an object but also at a distance. And this would be so if the animal is capable of perceiving through a medium, the latter being affected and moved by the object of perception, and the animal by the medium.

434^{b}29. For that which produces movement in respect of place produces a change up to a point, and that which has pushed something else brings it about that the latter pushes, the movement taking place through something intervening; the first thing that produces movement pushes without being pushed, and the last thing alone is pushed without pushing, while that which intervenes does both, there being many intervening things. So it is too with alteration, except that things are altered while remaining in the same place, e.g. if something were dipped in wax, the latter would be moved as far as the object was dipped; but a stone is not moved at all, while water is moved to a great distance; and air is moved to the greatest extent and acts and is affected if it persists and retains its unity.

435^{a}5. Hence too in the case of reflection it is better to say not that vision issuing from the eye is reflected back, but that the air is affected by shape and colour, as long as it retains its unity. Over a smooth surface it does retain this; hence it in turn produces movement in the organ of vision, just as if the impression on the wax had penetrated through to the further side.

CHAPTER 13

435^{a}11. It is apparent that the body of an animal cannot be simple; I mean, for example, composed of fire or air. For without touch it cannot have any other sense-perception$_A$; for every ensouled body is capable of touch, as we have said. Now the other elements, except for earth, could become sense-organs, but all the latter produce sense-perception$_A$ by perceiving through something else and through media. But touch occurs by directly touching objects; that too is why it has its name. Indeed even the other sense-organs perceive by touch, but through something else; touch alone seems to perceive through itself. Hence none of these elements could constitute the body of an animal.

435^{a}20. Nor can the body be composed of earth. For touch is, as it were, a mean between all objects of touch, and its organ is receptive of not only the qualities which are distinctive of earth but also heat and cold and all the other objects of touch. And for this reason we do not perceive with our bones and hair and such-like parts—because they are composed of earth. For this reason too plants have no sense-perception$_A$, because they are composed of earth.

But without touch it is not possible for any other {sense}
to exist, and this sense-organ is composed neither of earth
nor of any other of the elements.

435ᵇ4. It is apparent, therefore, that this is the only
sense$_A$ deprived of which animals must die. For, it is not
possible for anything which is not an animal to have this,
nor is there any other {sense} except this which something
which is an animal must have. And for this reason the
other objects of perception, e.g. colour, sound, and smell,
do not in excess destroy the animal, but only the sense-
organs, unless incidentally, e.g. if a push or a blow takes
place at the same time as the sound; by sights and smell too
other things may be set in motion which destroy by contact. And flavour too destroys only in so far as it happens
to be at the same time capable of coming into contact.
But an excess in objects of touch, e.g. hot, cold, or hard
things, destroys the animal. For excess in every object of
perception destroys the sense-organ, so that in the case
of objects of touch it will destroy touch, and by this the
animal is determined as such. For it has been shown that
without touch it is impossible for an animal to exist. Hence,
excess in objects of touch not only destroys the sense-
organ, but the animal also, because this sense$_A$ alone it
must have.

435ᵇ19. The other senses$_A$ the animal has, as we have said,
not for its existence, but for its well-being, e.g. it has sight
in order to see, because it lives in air and water, or, in
general, because it lives in something transparent; and it
has taste because of what is pleasant and painful, in order
that it may perceive these in food and have wants and be
moved accordingly; and hearing in order that something
may be indicated to it [and a tongue in order that it may
indicate something to another].

NOTES

BOOK ONE

CHAPTER 1

402ᵃ1. This is a typical Aristotelian beginning, setting out the importance of an inquiry into the nature of the soul. Such an inquiry is, in effect, a branch of biology. Here Aristotle connects the soul with *animal* life, which is, as he reveals later, an undue restriction, since the soul is the principle of life in general. This is how the soul was primarily understood by the Greeks from Homer onwards. Already here Aristotle introduces a distinction between the soul and the animal which has it—a distinction which is his version of the body–mind distinction.

402ᵃ10. On the face of it an inquiry into the essence of soul is like such inquiries elsewhere (the theory of such inquiries being given in the *Posterior Analytics*). We need to arrive at the relevant first principles inductively and then use demonstration to show that the attributes which belong to the things in the province of the science in question *must* belong to them. (The 'incidental properties' referred to here are not mere *accidents*, but those properties which follow from the thing's being what it is.) Aristotle goes on to raise the supposition that such inquiries may not be uniform in procedure (although he gives no hint *here* why not); and even if it is clear how to proceed in the present case, we still need to see from what first principles the inquiry must start. For different provinces of knowledge require different first principles; e.g. numbers, which involve 'discrete quantity', belong to a different field from planes, which involve 'continuous quantity', and thus in inquiring about them we need to start from different first principles.

The word here translated as 'first principle' is ἀρχή (*archē*). It means in general 'beginning' or 'source', and it has sometimes been necessary to translate it in some such general way. It has been translated as 'first principle' only when the technical meaning invoked here seems indicated. 'First principle' must be distinguished from 'principle', which, as made clear in the notes on the translation, is one way in which λόγος (*logos*) has been translated. There is, however, an obvious connexion between the two since a first principle is a *logos*; it sets out what is essential to the objects of the science in question.

402ª23. Aristotle mentions here further matters for preliminary inquiry—to which of the categories does the soul belong (Book II begins with the clear statement that it is substance), is it something potential or actual, is it a single thing either (*a*) numerically or (*b*) qualitatively?

402ᵇ3. With respect to (*b*) above, we cannot assume that 'soul' means the human soul, and we cannot assume that the soul of each species of thing is essentially the same. A common predicate may apply to each species in the same way or apply to them differently so that there is no single universal under which they can be subsumed in a straight-forward way. In effect, Aristotle is presenting as alternatives the possibilities that the predicate in question may be either univocal or equivocal.

402ᵇ9. With respect to (*a*) above, if the soul has parts should these be investigated first—or their functions—or the objects of these? Here for the first time Aristotle uses the '-*ikon*' construction referred to in the Notes on the Translation—'that which can perceive'. It must in this context be taken as referring to the faculty, in order to provide a parallel with the intellect (*v.* on 413ᵇ4). While the faculty of per-ception has an organ or organs which could also be referred to in this way, the intellect has none, according to Aristotle—a lack of parallelism which is never adequately dealt with by him.

402ᵇ16. As stated above, determining the essence of something enables one to deduce conclusions about what follows from such an essence—and conversely, knowledge of the attributes which so follow will help towards the determination of the essence. All this pre-supposes Aristotle's theory of demonstration and science.

403ª3. Aristotle again looks forward to his account of the soul in Books II and III. Are there any functions of the soul which do not involve the body? This is a crucial problem with respect to the intellect.

403ª10. If any function of the soul does not involve the body, then in that respect at least the soul is capable, logically, of having an existence independent of the body. (The 'logically' is strictly all that follows here.) The other alternative is that the body is always involved in any function or affection of the soul—in which case it could not, logically, have a separate existence.

Aristotle's comparison with the 'straight' is not very clear and suffers from compression. A straight line, as a mathematical entity, exists, according to Aristotle's general theory, only in abstraction from objects which are straight. What actually exists is the straight object and this could touch a bronze sphere. On the other hand, we can think of it as touching it *at a point* only if we think of the object and the sphere in so far as they exemplify the geometrical notions of straight line and point. Hence a straight line (the straight *qua* straight) can in an object touch a bronze sphere at a point; but it could not do this if it had a separate existence. Similarly, the soul could not exhibit functions involving the body if it had a separate existence.

403ᵃ16. It is not clear whether πάθη (*pathē*) in ᵃ16 refers, as suggested in the translation, merely to the affections of the soul, or perhaps even more specifically to emotions only, or whether it refers to *any* of its properties. πάθος (*pathos*) can be translated in any of these ways and is indeed translated as 'property' at 402ᵃ9, 403ᵃ3, and 403ᵇ10, 15. It is emotions which are mentioned by way of example in what follows, but sense-perception was referred to earlier at ᵃ7. It is probable that Aristotle has in mind here affections (i.e. forms of passivity or being affected) rather than properties in general, although later at ᵇ12 he reintroduces functions (ἔργα—*erga*) in addition to affections (*pathē*). παθήματα (*pathēmata*), which was used at ᵃ11 to mean affections, seems to mean what happens to us, i.e. sufferings, at ᵃ20, and is so translated. πάθος (*pathos*) has been translated as 'properties' or as 'affections' throughout.

Aristotle's observations about the dependence of states of mind on bodily conditions is noteworthy from a psychological point of view.

403ᵃ24. The word λόγος (*logos*) is here translated (somewhat unsatisfactorily) as 'principle'—meaning something objective, not verbal. The word suggests *form*, and since the soul is said later at the beginning of Book II to be form in the sense there specified, affections of the soul can be spoken of here in a similar way. Aristotle is trying to show that a definition of these will involve reference to material conditions, and hence that they are the province of the natural philosopher, who is concerned with the material.

403ª29. The person referred to here as the dialectician is one concerned to elucidate, for example, anger from the standpoint of our ordinary conception of it. (According to *Topics* I. 1 a dialectical argument may start from what is held to be so generally or by the parties to the discussion, i.e. from ordinary beliefs; *Rhetoric* II. 2–11 gives examples of the kind of account referred to here.) The distinctions which Aristotle draws at the end of the section are those between accounts of form, matter, and the compound of these two. Although Aristotle often associates 'form' with 'shape', the notion of 'form' is really very much wider than this. It is connected with that of 'essence', so that to give the form of a thing is often to give its essence, or to make clear its nature. Thus the form of a house has to do with its function, although in relation to the end in question this is dependent on the materials of which it is made.

403ᵇ7. Aristotle here embarks upon a digression which amounts to a classification of sciences. The student of nature or natural philosopher is really concerned with form in matter; he will investigate the properties of bodies of given kinds. We have already been told that the dialectician is concerned with form; we are now told that there is no one who is concerned with matter as such, no one, that is, who is concerned with the properties of matter, in contradistinction from properties of bodies composed of that matter. The physicist or natural philosopher, the craftsman, and the mathematician are all concerned with properties of bodies which are not strictly speaking separable from matter. The natural philosopher considers them as properties of bodies of a certain kind, the craftsman as properties which belong to bodies but not as consequences of their being bodies of that kind, and the mathematician as properties in abstraction, i.e. properties which are considered in abstraction from bodies although they are not really separable. Properties which are treated as really separable from matter are the concern of 'First Philosophy', which is tantamount to theology (cf. *Metaphysics* E 1 and Λ 6–10). Though πάθη (*pathē*) has been translated as 'properties' generally in this section, 'affections' is required at ᵇ12 to allow of the contrast with functions.

403ᵇ16. The affections of the soul to be studied here are to be considered as the student of nature or natural philosopher considers the properties of things, not as the mathematician does; they do not, that is to say, exist in abstraction.

CHAPTER 4

408^{a}34. Aristotle is considering the view of Xenocrates that the soul is a self-moving number. It should be noted that 'movement' covers change in general.

408^{b}5. Aristotle is arguing here that the movements or changes in question are changes in the bodily parts which either produce changes in the soul or are produced by it. (This does not in itself imply that the soul is something separate from the body, merely that the changes in the soul are different from mere bodily changes, whatever their exact status is.) In such circumstances it would be wrong to say that it is the *soul* which is, for example, angry, since the body is involved, just as it is in, for example, weaving or building. Hence the right thing to say is that the man or animal is the subject which is affected, e.g. in anger, or which is active, e.g. in thinking, not the soul.

Aristotle does not often live up to this remark. He speaks repeatedly of the senses judging, e.g. 418^{a}14, and also of the soul doing so, e.g. 427^{a}20; but, more fundamentally, the concept of a person or subject is generally missing from Aristotle's discussions of the problems in the philosophy of mind.

408^{b}18. Cf. III. 4 and 5. In effect Aristotle states once again that the intellect is an exception to what is generally the case with regard to the soul. It is substantial in its own right. To judge by III. 5, however, this applies only to the so-called active intellect.

The argument that follows seems to draw a parallel between the intellect and sight as far as concerns the effect of old age. It is claimed that neither is itself destroyed by old age; it is the body which is so affected. As it stands, the argument would suggest that there is no more reason for sight to be destroyed than for the same to happen to the intellect. But this is scarcely Aristotle's general view.

408^{b}24. It is here suggested that the failure of what is an affection of the composite of soul and body (Aristotle mentions thinking, loving, hating, and remembering) is due to the failure of the body. Aristotle then concludes with the assertion that the intellect itself is unaffected and is something more divine. There seems little here in the way of an argument for that conclusion.

CHAPTER 5

410ᵃ23. Cf. 416ᵇ33 for the suggestion that perception is a form of being affected, 429ᵃ13 ff. for a denial of this in the case of thinking, and 431ᵃ5 for a similar denial in the case of perception. The denials are due to a variety of factors—the recognition of the part played by judgement in both perception and thought, the fact that the intellect is said not to have an organ which can be affected, and the fact that the actualization of a potentiality (which both perception and thought are said to be) is initially subsumed under the category of passivity but is later differentiated from it.

BOOK II

CHAPTER 1

412ᵃ6. This cannot be considered an exhaustive summary of Aristotle's views on substance. The threefold division is introduced at *Metaphysics Z.* 3, in connexion with substance construed as subject of predication. Matter and form are further discussed in *Metaphysics H.* Matter is merely whatever can potentially receive form and is thus indefinite and indeterminate. Form gives it determinateness, and a particular sensible substance is a combination of a certain form with a certain matter. For the use of the words 'speak of' see on 412ᵃ22.

The distinction between the two ways in which form can be actuality is the distinction between *hexis* (ἕξις—state or capacity) and *energeia* (ἐνέργεια—activity or actuality, cf. 412ᵃ22 ff.), as the two forms of what is actual; a *hexis* must be distinguished from mere potentiality (*dunamis*—δύναμις) which manifests itself in movement or change (*kinēsis*—κίνησις) not activity (*v. Metaphysics Θ.* 6). *Hexis* is, though actual, potential in relation to *energeia*, since it is dispositional. The paradigm which Aristotle quotes is that of knowledge *qua* dispositional (*hexis*) as opposed to the exercise of knowledge (*energeia*). *Metaphysics Θ.* 2 says that things which have a rational part of the soul have a potentiality for opposites; in these the development of a *hexis* is possible, and there is a general implication in Aristotle that this comes about by practice. To apply this notion in the present case would restrict the soul to rational creatures, which Aristotle never intends. *Categories* 8^{b}26 ff. suggests that a *hexis* is just a more or less permanent state. This would for present purposes be too general a conception. If Aristotle cannot be said to be absolutely clear about the notion, we may certainly expect a *hexis* to manifest itself in a flexible and variegated way—which is not true of a *dunamis*.

412^{a}11. The belief that it is bodies especially that are substance is treated by Aristotle as a common view which provides a starting point for his inquiries concerning substance (v. *Metaphysics* 1028^{b}8 and *H*. 1).

Self-nourishment, etc., are not *the* defining characteristics of life, although they are necessary and sufficient conditions of anything being a living thing. Aristotle treats other functions, e.g. perception and thought, as forms of life in those creatures where they are to be found, and a correct view of his approach to the soul entails a realization of this point, even if he sometimes seems to contrast life with perception, etc. (cf. 413^{a}20 ff.).

Living natural bodies are composite substances, because they are a combination of matter and form, i.e. of bodily matter plus life (in its varying forms).

412^{a}16. The argument in this section is, to say the least, compressed. Aristotle assumes an association between the soul and life (an association which runs through the whole of Greek thought). The argument is presumably that since the kind of body with which we are concerned (i.e. animate body) is a natural one having life, and since to have life is to have soul, the soul cannot be a body (of this kind?), but must be related to the body as life is related to it. Aristotle produces as a reason for this conclusion that the body is not something which we can predicate of something else (it is *things* not words, in Aristotle's thought, that can be predicated or be subjects); the body is 'subject and matter'. Strictly speaking this identification of subject and matter is incorrect (cf. *Metaphysics Z*. 3), but there is in Aristotle a constant tendency to equate the subject/predicate distinction with the matter/form distinction (cf. 414^{a}14 and *Metaphysics* 1029^{a}21 ff.). This is presumably because *one* important answer to the question 'What is there? What are you talking about?' is 'Stuff' or 'Matter', and the form which that stuff takes can be thought of as something predicated of that stuff. It is not, however, the only answer.

Given that the soul is not body, and given that it is that in virtue of which a natural body has life, then the soul will be the form of a natural body which has the potentiality for life and hence, if form is substance, it will be substance in that sense. The body will have life potentially in the sense that it is the sort of body which can be living; the presence of soul makes it actually living.

'Substance is actuality.' Although Aristotle could maintain this generally, since substance is what exists primarily, the remark is true, given the classification of substances above, only of substance *qua* form. This is an indication that that classification is only rough.

412ª22. 'Actuality is so spoken of . . .': literally 'Actuality is said . . .', but we do not use 'say' in this way in English. This is a typical Aristotelian use; it is actuality (ἐντελέχεια—*entelecheia*) itself which is spoken of (or said) in two ways, not the word 'actuality'. It is the meaning (which is, in Aristotle's thought, the reference) of the word with which he is concerned, and one word may have more than one meaning or reference. To introduce the notion of *senses* of words would be to employ a notion which is foreign to Aristotle's theory of meaning, which is to the effect that the meaning of a word is a kind of thing. The force of the phrase under consideration is that actuality (= *hexis*, like knowledge, a disposition) and actuality (= *energeia*, like contemplation or the exercise of knowledge, an activity) are both spoken of *as actuality*, but, since they are different in the ways suggested, they are so spoken of in different ways. (There is in fact no 'so' in the Greek, but it has to be introduced in the English, since to say merely that actuality is spoken of in different ways would suggest a quite different interpretation from the right one. Similarly, it is necessary sometimes to introduce an 'as'—'that which is spoken of as . . .'.) We might prefer to say that the *word* 'actuality' is ambiguous; Aristotle would say that the two actualities are homonyms, i.e. they have the same name, but the definition which goes along with the name is different in each case (*v. Categories* 1). That is to say that the word picks out different although perhaps connected things. Aristotle was to adopt the view that very often one of the things so picked out is the primary reference of the word and that the others are derivative in some way from this. This became a central idea in his philosophy (*v. Metaphysics Γ*. 2, *Nicomachean Ethics* 1096ᵇ26 ff. for two important occurrences of this notion).

The soul is actuality only as *hexis*, i.e. in a dispositional way, since something may still be alive when asleep and not *doing* anything. In the individual the disposition is prior to its exercise, but Aristotle might have added that in nature in general what is actual is prior to what is potential; the exercise or actualization of dispositions depends on activity which is not dispositional, and Aristotle, perhaps invalidly, takes it to follow from this point that in general something actual must precede what is potential (cf. *Metaphysics* Θ. 8).

It is noteworthy that Aristotle believes that there is an activity of knowing, and that knowledge is not merely dispositional. In contemplating the objects of the intellect we are engaged in this activity, and it is this which the *Nicomachean Ethics* ultimately sets out as the end for the rational man.

'First actuality.' This has sometimes been interpreted as 'first in development' or 'first in importance'. In fact, as Alexander of Aphrodisias maintained, the first actuality is the *hexis*, which is presupposed by *energeia*. (For the difficulties in applying this notion to non-rational living things *v.* on 412^{a}6.)

412^{a}28. Aristotle here introduces organs as essential to any body capable of life.

412^{b}4. Aristotle offers not so much a formal definition of the soul (which, as he will indicate, is impossible since souls form a hierarchy, so preventing there being a genus with co-ordinate species), but the most general formula capable of covering all varieties of soul. Since it is a *hexis* of a body of the given kind, the two form a unity like that of the wax and the impression in it, i.e. a unity which is that of matter and form. For the various meanings of *unity* and *being* see *Metaphysics* Δ. 6 and 7 respectively. It is, properly speaking, the actuality or form of a thing in virtue of which it is said to be and to be one; form or actuality constitutes the principle of identity or individuation in the primary cases. Strictly speaking this implies that the primary cases cannot include anything that has matter, since the identity of a thing which has matter is not solely determined by its form. This is a central point in the argument of *Metaphysics* Z, and is brought out especially in chapter 11 of that book.

412^{b}10. Soul is therefore substance *qua* form or essence (as indicated by the use of *logos* here). Aristotle uses for essence his characteristic phrase τὸ τί ἦν εἶναι (*to ti ēn einai*). (How the phrase is to be construed literally is a matter for argument. It is often held that it should be construed as 'the what it was to be . . .', taking the εἶναι as dependent on the τί ἦν. I have, however, taken the view that the definite article and the εἶναι belong together as in Aristotle's characteristic use with a dative [cf. the example that immediately follows

here—τὸ πελέκει εἶναι (what it is for it to be an axe = the essence
of an axe.)] Given this, the question τί ἦν; [the imperfect tense
stressing perhaps the continuity of the thing] is now introduced in
the place of the noun in the dative, so producing the formula 'what
it is for it to be what it was'. However the phrase is to be construed
literally, there is no doubt that it means *essence*. [See also 429ᵇ19 and
430ᵇ28.])

Aristotle's selection of a tool, an axe, to provide an analogy with
the ensouled body reveals how close to the surface in this discussion is
the notion of *function*. The substance or essence of an axe *is* its function,
without which it would not be an axe. Like the Greeks in general,
Aristotle had no difficulty in thinking of a natural body as having a
function too (cf. *Nicomachean Ethics* 1097ᵇ22 ff.); this is part of his
general teleology. But, as he goes on to point out, there are differences
also between an axe and a natural body, which spoil the analogy.
This is the force of the words 'But as it is it is an axe'—the essence of
an axe is not its soul, since it does not have one, not being a living
thing.

'Homonymously'—an axe which could not serve its function, could
not cut, would be an axe only in name. It might be referred to as an
axe, but would not be one in the same way as an axe that can cut
would be one (*v*. on 412ᵃ22).

412ᵇ17. Aristotle now gives a superficially better analogy—that
between body/soul and organ/function. Sight is the function, i.e. the
essence, of the eye; it is its *hexis*. An eye which cannot function is an
eye only homonymously, like the axe mentioned above. Analogously,
perception is the function, i.e. essence or *hexis* of the body *qua* perceptive. The analogy is better because an eye has a function independently of our giving it one (which is not true of an axe). But it is
superficially better only, because while Aristotle takes it, in effect, as
analytic that an eye's function is sight (though he would not put the
point in these terms), an analytic proposition can be formulated with
respect to the general function of perception only by adding 'perceptive' to 'body'. This is because, while the eye has a function within
the bodily system, the body as a whole can be said to have functions
only in so far as its parts do.

Aristotle completes the analogy at 412ᵇ27, the intervening remark
being parenthetical. Its purpose is to explain the appropriate sense of
'potentially alive'. Seeds and fruit are potentially bodies which are
themselves potentially such as to live.

413ᵃ3. In so far as the soul consists merely of potential functions of parts of the body, it cannot have an existence separate from the body; but Aristotle leaves it an open question whether it is entirely like this. There may be certain psychical functions which have no bodily counterpart—although how this could be so is, to say the least, puzzling. It is clear that Aristotle is looking forward here to what he says about the active intellect in III. 5.

The remark about the possible analogy between the soul and a sailor in a ship (with which cf. Descartes, *Meditation* VI) is also puzzling, since the argument up to this point has tended completely in the opposite direction. It can be set down only as a lecturer's aside.

CHAPTER 2

413ᵃ11. Aristotle now begins again, with certain remarks on method. The procedure envisaged is clearly a dialectical one, involving induction. We have to start from experience, i.e. from what is familiar but unclear, and move to the clear appreciation of the principle involved. Experience may provide us with the facts, but a proper (real) definition will give the reason for these; so we argue from effects to causes—*a posteriori*. *Posterior Analytics* II. 11 shows how the reason for any given fact can be exhibited as the middle term of a syllogism in which the fact is stated as the conclusion; the middle term indeed connects certain facts, thus effecting an explanation of one of them. Aristotle gives here a geometrical example (*v.* Euclid, II. 14 and VI. 13). Given the following figure

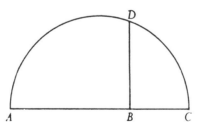

a square of area equal to that of a rectangle of sides *AB* and *BC* has a side equal in length to *BD* (finding this square is 'squaring'). But Euclid also shows that *AB* : *BD* :: *BD* : *BC* (*BD* is thus the mean proportional)—which can serve to explain the former fact.

413ª20 Aristotle starts again from the association of life and the soul. But life is said to be homonymous; there are many forms of it which are referred to by the same word, but these are not co-ordinate species of life, since the list of forms of life that follows constitutes a hierarchy. The higher functions are dependent on the lower, so that nutrition, decay, and growth, which were mentioned as conditions of life at 412ª14, are necessary conditions of other functions, since they are at the bottom of the hierarchy and higher forms depend on them. Something is alive if it has at least one of the functions mentioned in the list (counting nutrition, decay, and growth together as one).

413ª25. The principle which was stated in effect in the last section receives its confirmation in the case of plants, which have nutrition, decay, and growth, but no other function; they are alive and hence have a soul. It is in virtue of this that they grow in every part and in every direction.

413ᵇ1. A necessary condition of something's being an animal, on the other hand, is that it must have sense-perception.

413ᵇ4. Forms of sense-perception also constitute a hierarchy. Just as all living things must have the potentiality for self-nutrition, so all animals must have touch at least. How the hierarchy goes on is not altogether clear, but sight is presumably at the top.

435ᵇ4 ff. says that without touch animals must die—which sounds as if it means that an animal is causally dependent on touch for life. But even there Aristotle adduces as a consideration the fact that being an animal is determined by the possession of touch. In general Aristotle appears to mean that the possession of touch is a defining characteristic of an animal, but he sometimes puts the point in a misleading way.

αἴσθησις (aisthēsis), translated in ᵇ4 and ᵇ6 as 'perception' or 'sense-perception', can sometimes mean 'sense'; it *might* be so translated in ᵇ4, and has been so translated in ᵇ7. For a sense is a form of perception. I have translated the word in one of these ways wherever possible, but at 423ª3, in connexion with touch, 'sensation' is the natural translation. The *concept* of aisthēsis is in Aristotle, as with the Greeks generally, ambiguous between the concepts of sensation and perception (*v.* my *Sensation and Perception*, ch. 1 for a discussion of this point).

'Nutritive faculty.' Aristotle here uses the '-*ikon*' terminology referred to in the notes on the translation and on 402ᵇ9; it is literally 'that which can nourish', etc. The translation in terms of 'faculty' is sometimes desirable and at other times, e.g. at 402ᵇ13 and 413ᵇ12, it is unavoidable. But there are equally passages, e.g. 417ᵇ16, 418ᵃ3, 419ᵃ18, 426ᵃ11, 16, 429ᵃ17, 431ᵃ4, where such a translation is undesirable, what is referred to being the sense-organ, the animal, or something indeterminate. (It is noteworthy that in the lines following 429ᵃ17 the translation 'faculty' becomes necessary, despite its undesirability at 429ᵃ17 itself.) It is probable that Aristotle was not himself aware of the ambiguity of the terminology, as such shifts in sense indicate.

The circumstances referred to in the last sentence of this section are those mentioned in the first two sentences (the intervening sentence being parenthetical). The later discussion referred to is probably that to be found in III. 12.

413ᵇ11. Aristotle's questions put forward in this section about whether each faculty 'is a soul or a part of a soul' amount merely to whether in different creatures a faculty can exist by itself, and if it cannot, i.e. if it constitutes merely part of the soul, how it is related to the other parts—whether, for example, it exists separately from them in its bodily location.

413ᵇ16. The remarks which open this section do not seem to be directly relevant to the problem raised in the previous section; they merely indicate that both plants and animals are capable of division so that the parts retain the functions of the whole. Hence their soul is 'potentially many'. This is not the same problem as whether a *faculty* (or a part of the soul *in this sense*) can have separate existence. The concluding remarks return to this problem and maintain the interdependence of sense-perception, imagination, and desire. There is a lengthier discussion of these points in Chapter 3, where at 415ᵃ10 the universal coincidence of perception and imagination is disputed.

ὄρεξις (*orexis*), translated 'desire', seems to be the general word covering different forms of desire, including wishing. ἐπιθυμία (*epithumia*), translated 'wanting' is sometimes used in a general way but is at 432ᵇ6 attributed to the irrational part of the soul, just as wishing (βούλησις—*boulēsis*) belongs to the rational part (cf. 433ᵃ17 ff.), on the assumption that the soul has such parts.

The assertion that pain and pleasure involve wanting (to be rid of something or to have it) seems correct on the whole, although whether it amounts to a conceptual necessity is a matter for argument. On the other hand, the assertion that the existence of sense-perception necessarily implies the existence of pleasure and pain has no claim to conceptual necessity and seems dubious except perhaps as an empirical generalization. Aristotle is perhaps led to make the statement because *aisthēsis* means for him all forms of sensibility covering both perception and sensation. Hence he takes it to follow that, where one form of sensibility—perception—is present, the others must be present as well.

413ᵇ24. This is another reference to the ambiguous role of the intellect in Aristotle's scheme. Cf. 403ᵃ6 ff., 408ᵇ18 ff., 413ᵃ6.

413ᵇ27. The only reasons that Aristotle has given for the inseparability of parts of the soul are the brief remarks about the interdependence of perception, imagination, and desire in 413ᵇ16 ff. He has not yet presented much of an argument for his conclusion. But see further Chapter 3.

Aristotle provides a sample argument to show that the parts of the soul differ at any rate in definition or essence, by taking the cases of perception and belief or judgement. Since perceiving and believing or judging are clearly different, he argues, the abilities to perceive and believe or judge, i.e. the faculties, must be different. His account of the status of belief is not altogether forthright, but *v.* 427ᵇ16 ff. and 428ᵃ16 ff.

413ᵇ32. If the text is correct Aristotle's statement that animals can have only one faculty is, to say the least, loose; it is surely not possible for an *animal* to have just one faculty (cf. 414ᵃ32 ff.).

The further discussion referred to is perhaps III. 12 and 13.

414ᵃ4. The Greek text for this paragraph contains in fact one long sentence, the construction of which is open to dispute. It is, however, best taken as an argument which contains a number of remarks as premisses; the last words state the conclusion.

Aristotle's procedure is in effect to make distinctions between senses of 'by means of which' (although his theory of meaning prevents his putting the matter in that way; *v.* earlier on 412ᵃ22). He does this by means of parallel references to 'life and perception', 'knowledge', and 'health'. In each case there is a distinction to be made between what is, in effect, the formal cause and the material cause of each. (One of the troubles with the examples is that the soul has to be the material cause of our knowing but the formal cause of our living and perceiving, but as long as it is realized that the distinction between form and matter is a relative one this should not cause too much difficulty.) Aristotle then makes explicit the point that knowledge and health are the forms of that which is capable of knowledge and health respectively, and he uses a variety of synonymous terms for the purpose—shape (*morphē—μορφή*), form (*eidos—εἶδος*) and principle (*logos—λόγος*)—adding 'as it were activity (*energeia*) of the recipient' (i.e. of that which receives knowledge and health). The point is presumably that knowledge and health can each be construed as a *hexis* (for which *v.* on 412ᵃ6) of this recipient. The relation of activity or actuality to potentiality is in Aristotle always parallel or analogous to that of form to matter (*v.* e.g. *Metaphysics* Θ. 6). That activity takes place in the object affected is a general principle which Aristotle puts forward in many places (cf. 426ᵃ2 ff. and for the case of change in general *Physics* 202ᵃ13 ff.). The point is that activity is an actualization of a potentiality and this is brought about by a cause which is itself a form of activity. The principle stated thus provides a pattern in terms of which Aristotle sees all processes.

The penultimate step in the argument makes the point that the soul is that by means of which we live, perceive, and think *in the primary way*, and it is inferred from this that it is form or principle, not matter or subject. It is not clear altogether what are the grounds for the statement about the soul except the kind of understanding of what the soul is that has been implicit in the whole discussion so far. The primacy of form over matter in the determination of what a thing is is argued for in *Metaphysics* Z, esp. ch. 17. For the identification of matter and subject *v.* on 412ᵃ16 ff.

414ᵃ14. Aristotle here repeats in effect the opening remarks of Chapter 1, except that he now associates (as he does generally) matter with potentiality and form with actuality. This allows him, given the identification of the soul as form, to assert that the soul is the actuality of a body. It is so, of course, in the sense specified at 412ᵃ22.

414ᵃ19. Aristotle now sums up his conclusions, agreeing with those who say that the soul depends for its existence on the body without being a body (cf. the view that the soul is an attunement of the bodily parts, referred to and argued against by Plato, *Phaedo* 85 e ff.), but disagreeing with those (perhaps Pythagoreans, cf. 407ᵇ13 ff., not translated here) who give no account of the nature of the body to which the soul is supposed to be fitted or of the way in which the connexion takes place.

CHAPTER 3

414ᵃ29. The potentialities mentioned here are the various faculties. Aristotle begins by speaking of potentialities and proceeds immediately to a use of the '-*ikon*' terminology. Although he speaks of 'existing things' he means of course 'living things'. The reference 'as we have said' is to 413ᵇ32. In Book II the faculties have been listed at 413ᵃ23 and 413ᵇ12, but desire has not appeared in the list explicitly although it has been referred to in other ways; it has also appeared in an incomplete list of functions of the soul in Book I at 411ᵃ26 ff. (not here translated).

414ᵃ32. This passage repeats what was said in the latter half of the paragraph begining 413ᵇ16, except that it adds further details. Desire is explicitly classified here into wishing (βούλησις—*boulēsis*), passion (θυμός—*thumos*), and wanting (ἐπιθυμία—*epithumia*); the first is said at 432ᵇ5 to belong to the rational part of the soul if the theory that the soul has parts is accepted, the other two to the irrational part. At all events it appears that Aristotle conceives of wishing as something rational in a way in which the other two kinds of desire are not. Aristotle also seems to connect pleasure with irrational wants particularly. The way in which he does this here is not above criticism; strictly speaking, in order to attain his desired conclusion that sense-perception implies desire, he should state the matter the other way round—that the pleasant is that which we want, rather than that wanting is a desire for what is pleasant. On the other hand, Aristotle does not commit the fallacy that we always want *pleasure* as such; it is the pleasant that we are said to want. For the connexion of sense-perception with pleasure and pain see the note on 413ᵇ16.

414ᵇ6. Aristotle here puts forward another argument for the connexion between sense-perception and desire—an argument distinct from that already given. It is not a very good argument; it is obscurely put and has been subject to varying interpretations. For example, the words 'incidentally of other objects of perception' have been taken as saying that living things are nourished incidentally by other objects of perception than those which are objects of touch. This cannot be right. The bracketing adopted in the O.C.T. suggests that the sense concerned with food is incidentally one for other objects; this suggestion may not be positively wrong, since the sense in question is touch, but it cannot be what Aristotle intends. The argument seems in fact to run as follows: 'We have been told already that all animals have touch. It is touch that is concerned with food or nourishment, since it is the dry, moist, hot, and cold which are responsible for nourishment, and touch is concerned essentially with these and only incidentally with other objects of perception, e.g. sound, colour, and smell. Touch is the sense concerned with food, because these other objects do not nourish, while flavour, the object of taste, is itself an object of touch (since, as will be said later, taste is a form of touch). Hunger and thirst are forms of wanting objects of touch, i.e. the dry and hot, wet and cold, and flavour. Hence, having touch (and thereby concern with objects of touch) implies desire (at least in the form of hunger and thirst).' Unfortunately the conclusion does not seem in the least to follow. It is in fact difficult to see what valid argument *could* be produced to show that there must always be a connexion between sense-perception and desire; the possibility of a creature which perceives things without having any desire to have them or to be rid of them seems at least conceivable, although it may be admitted that such a creature would not fit into Aristotle's teleological scheme. Its perceptions would serve no function.

For essential and incidental objects of perception see II. 6 generally; and for senses perceiving objects of other senses incidentally see 425^{a}30 ff. For taste as a form of touch see 422^{a}8.

414^{b}16. The doubts about imagination are both about its nature (v. III. 3) and about the extent to which animals have it (v. III. 11).

Aristotle makes very little distinction in the *De Anima* between the faculty of thought (τὸ διανοητικόν—*to dianoētikon*) and the intellect (νοῦς—*nous*). If a distinction is to be made it is that the former is discursive, while the latter is not necessarily so; it may be intuitive, and as such it is 'always true'.

The 'anything else . . . superior to man' includes any divine intelligences, e.g. the intelligences so called of *Metaphysics Λ.* 8 which are responsible for the movement of the heavenly bodies, and God himself.

414^{b}20. From here until the end of the chapter Aristotle makes explicit certain difficulties about the definition of the soul which were implicit in I. 1, especially at 402^{b}3 ff. The difficulties arise out of the hierarchical arrangement of the faculties already mentioned (i.e. the fact that anything which has intellect must have perception, and anything that has this must have self-nutrition, etc.), and it is this too which makes the situation over definition 'clear'. The situation is like that over the definition of figure since the possibility of four- or five- or more-sided figures depends on that of three-sided figures. The difficulty in fact arises whenever a general term covers things that form a progression or hierarchy, as Aristotle makes clear at 414ᵇ29, e.g. numbers (*Metaphysics* 999ᵃ6 ff.), or forms of constitution (*Politics* 1275ᵃ35 ff.), or categories of being (*Nicomachean Ethics* 1096ᵃ17 ff.). There was a similar Platonic reservation about there not being a single Form of number.

It is to be noted that Aristotle does not say that it is impossible to produce *any* definition of figure and soul; the point is that if you do, it will not be informative about figures and souls. These are not correlative species under a genus; there is no proper genus, just as there is no proper genus of being over and above the categories. An account of figure in general or soul in general (just as for being in general) will be uninformative about figures or souls, not just in the way that any general definition is uninformative about the details of the things to which it is applied, but also because it will omit the crucial point that figures and souls form a progression. This would be true of Aristotle's initial account of the soul in Chapter 1 if taken by itself.

414ᵇ25. Given the foregoing, Aristotle emphasizes the unfruitfulness of trying to provide a general definition of the soul rather than concentrating on the particular faculties, each possible combination of which constitutes an 'indivisible species', i.e. a basic type of soul.

414ᵇ28. Here the parallel between figures and souls is worked out with reference to the development of the series—what is earlier or in some sense prior being presupposed by (existing potentially in) what comes next. Aristotle then draws the moral.

414ᵇ33. Aristotle finally comes back to the way in which different faculties (which in different animals may constitute different kinds of soul) form a hierarchy. A similar hierarchy exists for the different senses, at least in that the others are dependent on touch.

CHAPTER 4

415ᵃ14. Aristotle here answers a number of questions set out in I. 1 about the order of procedure. One first has to grasp the essence of each faculty or kind of soul and then go on to its essential properties, etc.

Again, when concerned with faculties (i.e. potentialities) we must first deal with the corresponding activities (i.e. actualities), since actuality is logically prior (i.e. prior in definition) to potentiality. That is to say that what can be so is intelligible only in terms of what actually is so—we can understand what it is for something to be potentially so only if we already understand what it is for it to be actually so. In the order of nature potentiality must precede what is actual in an individual, since what is F can only come from what can be F, but even this possibility presupposes *some* actual F (cf. 431ᵃ2 and *Metaphysics* Θ. 8).

Finally Aristotle says that the study of the objects of the activities must come before that of the activities themselves. In what follows immediately Aristotle does not strictly carry this out. The reason may be that the word translated 'nourishment' (τροφή—*trophē*) can mean either food (the object) or nutrition (the activity). Because he uses this word together with that for reproduction at the beginning of the next section he is led to consider the activity or function rather than the object. I have translated the word variously as 'food', 'nutrition', and 'nourishment'; the last perhaps preserves something of the ambiguity of the Greek.

415ᵃ22. Nourishment and reproduction are put together as the basic biological functions. In fact no previous justification of this has been provided; nor is it clear why they are both functions of one faculty, the nutritive.

The words 'in order that they may partake of the everlasting and divine' suggest the doctrine put forward by Diotima in Plato's *Symposium* 206 e ff.; but it is to be noted that what Aristotle has in mind is something entirely in accordance with nature—a nature in which there may be nevertheless exceptions to the normal processes. In this connexion the normal process is preservation of the species, not the individual (cf. *De Generatione et Corruptione* II. 11 and *De Generatione Animalium* II. 1).

The reference to the two uses of 'that for the sake of which' is a characteristic parenthesis which is repeated at 415ᵇ20–21.

415ᵇ8. Aristotle now begins a further analysis of the nature of the soul in terms of the doctrine of the four causes (cf. *Physics* II. 3). Three of the causes (or meanings of 'cause') are here mentioned—the efficient, final, and formal causes. The fourth, the material cause, is

not mentioned as it is not relevant to the soul as the form of the body.
The coincidence of the other three is often maintained by Aristotle
(*v. e.g. Metaphysics* 1041ª27 ff.). Aristotle's doctrine is normally referred to as the doctrine of the four causes, but it must be admitted
that 'cause' is not an altogether happy translation of αἰτία (*aitia*),
given the modern connotation of that term. To give the *aitia* of a
thing is to give some kind of reason why it is so, and Aristotle's
doctrine amounts to a classification of such kinds of reason. Owing,
however, to its etymological origins, the word '*aitia*' also suggests the
notion of responsibility, so that to give the *aitia* of a thing is also to
suggest something about what is responsible for it in some sense.

415b12. The soul is the cause of life *qua* form or essence of a living
body; it is the actuality of the body which is potentially living. It is so,
in that to speak of the soul is to speak of the various *hexeis* that the
living body can possess. These *hexeis* or functions are forms of life and
constitute life in a body of the appropriate kind. It is in this sense that
the soul determines what it is for a body of an appropriate kind to be
living.

415b15. The soul is the final cause also—the purpose for which natural
or living bodies function, nature being throughout teleological. The
phrase 'instruments for soul' should not be construed as meaning
instruments employed by soul, since if the soul is the end there can
be no suggestion of the soul, in this sense, acting as agent. It cannot
be said that the sense in which the soul is the end is very clear. Presumably the point is that the eye, for example, functions in order that
there may be perception, i.e. the end is the functioning of the organ—
and so on for the other faculties. Hence the functioning of a living
body is the end for which it exists, and for which nature uses it.

415b21. The soul is also the efficient cause in the sense that it is due
to it that living things move when they do, or at least change, grow,
and decay. The soul is thus the sufficient condition of these things
when there is the appropriate body. This is what Aristotle seems to
mean, although it is difficult to see how the soul, if it is a set of dispositions, could be more than a necessary condition of the actual
functioning of the body. Something fully actual is required as the
sufficient condition, i.e. to bring about the actualization of the dispositions. See III. 5 for what seems to be Aristotle's final position on
this issue.

The statement that perception is thought to be a form of alteration, though often repeated, is eventually contradicted at 431ᵃ5.

415ᵇ28. The criticism of Empedocles is based simply on the point that he misunderstood the nature of plants and the part played by the soul in them. Aristotle holds that the natural movement of fire is upwards, that of earth downwards, but that this is so only in the universe at large, where an upwards movement means movement from the centre to the circumference (cf. *Physics* 208ᵇ8 ff.). Relative to us, terms like 'up' and 'down' are purely relative in meaning, 'up' meaning above our heads. Thus Aristotle argues that as the roots of plants are like the head in men, being where food is taken in, 'up' for them is in effect what 'down' is for us. But what this really amounts to is that Empedocles did not see what roots are; nor did he see that the different tendencies in plants need a principle of organization.

416ᵃ9. The view referred to here is probably that of Heraclitus at least. The supposition in question depends on a simple but misplaced analogy. Once again Aristotle makes reference to the necessity for a principle of organization in growth, which is not apparent in fire.

416ᵃ19. Aristotle resumes the discussion of nutrition and makes general remarks about the kind of process that nutrition is, wherever it is to be found, basing his remarks on a common view that nutrition depends on opposites or contraries. Aristotle qualifies the thesis by saying that the opposites or contraries in question must be capable of increase, that the relation need not be reciprocal since, e.g., water is food for fire but not vice versa, and that the process which the view has in mind is one which takes place especially 'in the simple bodies'. The last remark is far from clear and little has led up to it except the statement that water is food for fire (perhaps because you need wood that is not too dry to keep a fire going); in this last kind of 'feeding' the things concerned are elements and therefore presumably simple bodies. Aristotle may be putting a limitation on the view under discussion or maintaining that it applies only to basic processes which may of course underlie other more obvious forms of nutrition. Another possibility is that the words 'simple bodies' do not refer to the elements so much as to what Aristotle sometimes calls 'homoeomerous bodies', i.e. bodies, like flesh or tissues generally, whose parts are like the whole and which are therefore simple in structure.

416ᵃ29. Aristotle goes on to mention conflicting views on this matter in terms of the like-like/like-unlike dichotomy. The suggestion that what is fed is not affected by the food seems odd. Ross (ed. of *De Anima*, ad loc.) suggests that what is fed is not changed *in character*, although it grows, while the food is changed by the feeding process.

416ᵇ3. A reconciliation between the opposed views is now offered by means of the distinction between undigested and digested food. But exactly how this provides a complete reconciliation is still not clear, given all the objections in the previous section.

416ᵇ9. On the face of it, this remark should provoke qualification of the earlier remark about fire being fed by water. It does suggest that Aristotle was not there consistently talking about the ordinary cases of nutrition.

416ᵇ11. Food is a substance. It can cause growth, but the notions of being food and being capable of causing growth are different. Food as such enables the plant or animal to maintain the substance of what is fed, i.e. its body. Similarly the plant or animal can reproduce another substance like itself. Growth occurs in so far as the food is also capable of causing growth.

416ᵇ20 ff. It seems paradoxical at first sight to say that it is the soul (i.e. the primary form of soul, the nutritive faculty) which feeds the body with food, though it follows perhaps from what Aristotle has said about the soul's being the efficient cause of motion, alteration, and growth. Nevertheless a more accurate statement might be that it is the animal or plant which feeds and reproduces itself; the soul is that with which it does so in another sense of 'that with which' from that in which food is so (cf. the remarks at 414ª4 ff., although what follows here at 416ᵇ25 ff. makes yet another distinction between things with which one feeds—a distinction of a quite different kind).

416ᵇ25. The instrument of nourishment is not just the food, but the natural heat of the body. This is set in motion by the soul (and is in this respect like the hand) and it itself moves the food which (thereby like a rudder) is merely passive. The analogy is, however, misleading and mystifying; for whereas we may consciously move the hand to move the rudder, we do not consciously move the natural heat, and to say that the soul does so is not helpful both for the reasons given above on 416ᵇ20 and because it still leaves the process a mystery. The truth is that Aristotle is far from clear about the relationship between the conceptual framework involved when we speak of ourselves or animals (not to mention plants) doing things, and that involved when we speak of the causal processes underlying all this.

The 'appropriate work' does not seem to exist, although *De Somno* $456^{b}6$ refers to a work on nutrition.

CHAPTER 5

$416^{b}32$. The previous statement that perception is a form of being moved and affected is to be found at $415^{b}24$. The 'some' mentioned here are probably Democritus and perhaps Empedocles. Aristotle discusses this matter in *De Generatione et Corruptione* I. 7.

$417^{a}2$. It is noteworthy that the same word αἴσθησις (*aisthēsis*) must be translated differently as 'perception' and 'sense' in successive occurrences, and that by 'sense' is clearly meant *sense-organ*. (Aristotle frequently uses the word for a sense in order to speak of a sense-organ.) The problem here is thus why we do not ever perceive, through a given sense-organ, that very sense-organ itself, despite the fact that it contains the same elements of which 'external objects' are composed and which act as objects of perception either in themselves or in virtue of properties that they happen to have. (The reference to 'external objects' is especially noteworthy; it indicates that the idea of a world external to ourselves or our body—not just different or apart from ourselves or our body—with the implication that we are somehow *inside*, is to be met with as early as Aristotle. The idea, erroneous and misleading as it is, has persisted throughout most of Western philosophy, but it is not altogether clear what promotes it in Aristotle himself; he pays very little attention to those aspects of the privacy of experience which have generally led to it.)

Aristotle's solution of his problem is also not very clear. His suggestion is that the faculty of sense-perception is a mere potentiality which needs to be actualized. Since the faculty is something which belongs essentially to an organ (cf. $424^{a}24$ ff.), the actualization can take place only because of something 'external'; thus the perception of the sense-organ itself by its own faculty does not occur (this being what is meant by the words 'the perception does not occur'). The solution presupposes Aristotle's scheme of things according to which the actualization of a potentiality must always be due to something else which is in some sense actual. But even if this is accepted, Aristotle has given no reason for the assumption that if something must have what is in effect an external cause it must also have an external object (leaving out of consideration the shift in the sense of 'external' that this involves). It can surely only be a conceptual point that if we were in some way aware of our sense-organs in using them this would not count as perception (cf. the analogous difficulties at $425^{b}17$ ff.).

417ᵃ9. The reference to potentiality in the last section leads Aristotle to make general remarks about actuality and potentiality which take him through the rest of the chapter. The distinction between actual and potential knowing has already been made at $412^{a}22$ ff. Aristotle here extends the distinction to cover perception and its object.

417ᵃ14. Aristotle should not be taken as saying here that being affected (or moved) and acting are literally the same thing, although the same thing may be said to be affected and to act, and at the same time. In other words, one occurrence may be viewed both as a case of being affected and as a case of acting (cf. on $425^{b}26$). Aristotle goes on to give as a reason for his view the fact or claimed fact that movement is a form of incomplete activity (cf. $431^{a}4$ ff., *Physics* $201^{b}31$, *Metaphysics* $1048^{b}23$ ff.). The assertion that movement can be construed as a form of incomplete activity involves the idea that movements should be thought of not as simple occurrences but as made by something. This is indeed characteristic of Aristotle's general view of movement and is an integral part of his teleological approach to it. Thus typical examples which he gives of movement are building and walking, odd though these examples may seem at first sight. Apart from any general doubts that one might have about all this, the difficulty that it presents in the case under consideration is that it does not *explain* why being moved is the same as acting; for this to be the case being moved would have to be equated with making a movement, and whether this is possible is the whole point at issue.

What Aristotle means when he says that movements *qua* activities are incomplete is not altogether clear. *Nicomachean Ethics* $1174^{a}13$ ff. suggests that movements are incomplete because they take time and imply an end separate from them. Thus activities proper need not take time and need not have an end which is extrinsic. *Metaphysics* $1048^{b}23$ ff. presents a criterion which has some connexion with this— that with activities it is the case that, e.g., 'at the same time one sees and has seen, understands and has understood, thinks and has thought'. The exact significance of this criterion and its consistency with the actual examples used present difficulties (for which see

J. L. Ackrill in *New Essays on Plato and Aristotle*, edited by Renford Bambrough, pp. 121–41), although perhaps *some* of the difficulties can be removed by the recognition that the distinction between activity and movement, like that between form and matter, or actuality and potentiality, is relative (even if Aristotle did not himself accept all the implications of this). At all events it would be a mistake to take what is said at *Metaphysics* 1048ᵇ23 ff. as providing *the* criterion for the distinction between activity and movement. The incompleteness of movement must primarily be explained in other ways—by the reference or lack of reference to a separate end or (cf. 431ª7 and *Physics* 201ᵇ31 ff.) in terms of the completeness or otherwise of that which manifests the activity or movement. 431ª7 thus speaks of activity proper as the activity of the complete or completed—the activity arises out of the thing's nature, out of its *hexis* (cf. 417ᵇ2 ff.).

Aristotle goes on to state the principle mentioned in the notes on the previous section, that change must be due to something actual; he uses this to reconcile the opposed positions over whether what affects another thing must be like it or unlike it. Affecting something is construed as a process of assimilation; the kind of being affected said to be involved in sense-perception turns out to be like this.

417ª21. Here further distinctions are made with reference to the application of the potential/actual dichotomy. The two kinds of potentiality correspond to *dunamis* and *hexis* respectively (cf. on 412ª6). Something has a given *dunamis* because of the kind of thing it is. Physical things have potentialities (*dunameis*) for natural movements in a given direction; but, as noted on 412ª6, things which have a soul and, in particular, reason have a potentiality for opposites, the disposition to one of which is eliminated and the other reinforced in the process of training or education. (Thus according to *Nicomachean Ethics* 1103ª34 ff. a man becomes just by doing just things.) This idea is invoked here in speaking of 'frequent changes from an opposite disposition'. Thus a particular *hexis* is developed, the exercise of which is activity. (The word here translated as 'disposition' is in fact '*hexis*'. Either of the initial potentialities might have become a settled *hexis*: what has to be achieved is the abandonment of the tendency to one of them.)

For knowing as something active see on 412ª22. Contemplation is for Aristotle not just a passive awareness. It should also be noted that its object is a particular individual ('this particular A'). Cf. *Metaphysics* 1087ª15 ff.

417ᵇ2. While the structure of this passage is not very clear, it is evident enough that Aristotle is using the distinctions made in the previous section to cast light on further distinctions relevant to the forms of being affected which were noted at 417ᵃ14 ff. There is (a) straightforward change from one state to its opposite—which can be viewed as a kind of destruction of one of two contraries; (b) the actualization of what is already potentially such. The latter is 'either not an alteration . . . or a different kind of alteration'. This applies to activity in virtue of a *hexis* (e.g. understanding) as well as to movement arising from a *dunamis* (e.g. building, if this is to be taken, as is usual with Aristotle's use of the example, as a movement). The actualization of a *hexis* is not itself teaching, Aristotle says, while learning as a result of teaching, on the other hand, is not, strictly speaking, a case of being altered; it is in fact the acquisition of a *hexis*.

417ᵇ16. In the case of perception the *hexis* is born with us. The first change, i.e. the transition from *dunamis* to *hexis*, does not have to be acquired; it takes place on conception. We do not have to learn to perceive; we can perceive already when born and our capacity is then, *qua capacity*, like knowledge. The main way in which there is not a parallel between knowledge and perception is that the latter requires 'external objects' (*v.* on 417ᵃ2); these are particular, while the objects of knowledge are universals and 'somehow in the soul itself'. Moreover, Aristotle connects this with the fact that thinking is in a sense voluntary, while perception is dependent on there being objects for it.

There are several difficulties in this:

(a) Aristotle speaks as if there is a capacity for perception, a *hexis* which presupposes its acquisition like any other *hexis*, but not in this case through experience. This seems to suggest that it at least makes sense to speak of the acquisition of such a capacity; but it surely makes no sense, except in that the capacity may be allowed to manifest itself, as is the case when people are given the power to see through surgical operations, e.g. for congenital cataract. It does, indeed, make sense to speak of acquiring a capacity for seeing something *as* such and such; but this *can* come through experience. All this suggests that there is something wrong with Aristotle's attempt to apply the *dunamis–hexis–energeia* scheme to perception and to anything parallel with it. In order to apply the scheme Aristotle has also to assume that there is an activity of perceiving and knowing, and the fact that, as *we* use the words 'perceive' and 'know', there cannot be said to be such an activity is connected with its making no sense to speak of acquiring a capacity for such. To say that when a child is born he can, in some sense, see is not to say that he has a capacity for doing something called 'seeing'.

(b) To make a point which is in a way connected with the foregoing —it is noteworthy that when Aristotle comes to distinguish between perception and knowledge in terms of whether and when they are 'open to us', he has to speak of thinking rather than knowing; for knowledge is, just as much as perception, dependent on its objects (you cannot know what does not exist or what is not the case). There is a constant tendency for Aristotle to run thinking and knowing together, as his invocation of an 'activity' sense of 'knowing' reveals.

(c) The sense in which the universals, which are said to be objects of knowledge, are in the soul by no means justifies the conclusion drawn; nor is it obvious that the objects of knowledge and perception can be differentiated in this way. First, it has already been implied at 417ª29 that actual knowledge, i.e. contemplation, may be of a particular (cf. *Metaphysics* 1087ª15 ff., which claims that potential knowledge is of universals, actual knowledge of particulars). Second, 429ª22 ff. and 431ᵇ26 ff. say that forms are in the soul because the intellect is potentially its objects. But, *in that way*, so are the senses their objects; and, as discussion of these later passages will show, it is not clear even to Aristotle that the objects of the intellect and the senses are necessarily always different. On the other hand, there is a sense in which some objects of *thought* may be said to be in the soul in a way in which at any rate some objects of perception are not; that is to say that the objects in question may exist only as *intentional objects*. But this is not true of all objects of thought and it does not apply in any case to objects of knowledge.

Aristotle's confusions in this passage are evident enough, but they are endemic in his thought.

417ᵇ29. After making the *dunamis/hexis* distinction once again and maintaining that the ability to perceive is a *hexis*, Aristotle says that there is no word to mark the distinction between the actualizations of a *dunamis* and a *hexis* respectively. We must therefore put up with words suggesting that perception is a form of being altered or affected, since no name exists for the exact process in question (i.e. the actualization of a *hexis* as opposed to that of a *dunamis*). Aristotle's unwillingness here to introduce technical terminology is noteworthy.

418ª3. Aristotle sums up the kind of process involved in perception. He has not previously maintained explicitly the view put forward here, but it is implicit in the previous discussion and the reconciliation of sides in the like/unlike dispute has been suggested at 417ª14 ff.

The question arises what exactly it is that is potentially such as the object of perception is actually. The expression 'that which can perceive' seems to be used quite generally in the previous passages, but it could be argued that it may be used to speak of the faculty of perception here. On the other hand, in asserting the principle with respect to the individual senses at 422ª7, 422ᵇ15, 423ᵇ30 ff. he clearly means it to apply to the sense-organ. 431ª4 is on the face of it ambiguous. 431ᵇ23 applies it to the sense (as a parallel with knowledge), but 431ᵇ26 appears to apply it to the faculty. 425ᵇ26 says that the activity of the object of perception is the same as that of the sense. 426ª15 ff. repeats the remark except that the phrase 'that which can perceive' is substituted for 'sense'. It is not clear whether these passages assert the doctrine with which we are concerned, although what they say clearly has a connexion with it. But other than this the only passage which runs directly counter to the view that the principle holds of the *sense-organ* is 431ᵇ26, and this comes from a passage which provokes other doubts. It would seem, therefore, that what Aristotle usually meant to say was that the sense-organ is potentially such as the object of perception is actually.

It is a principle which, like the parallel one that the sense-organ receives the sensible form without the matter, which is introduced at 424ª17 (for which see the notes ad loc.), seems applicable only to certain senses. Indeed Aristotle himself mentions it in discussing the special senses only in the cases of smell, taste, and touch. In certain cases the sense-organ may take on the properties of the object, and as a piece of the physiology of the senses this seems unexceptionable. But the eye, as Themistius pointed out, does not become white when we look at something white. *De Sensu* 438ᵇ26 ff. has an argument which maintains that the organ of smell, being near to the brain (according to Aristotle the cooling system of the body), is cold and therefore potentially hot, which is appropriate to smells which are associated with heat by way of smoke. This is a very special, not to say odd, argument, but it indicates the kind of thing that Aristotle had in mind. It is very unclear what he would have said in this way about the eye and ear. Nevertheless, it *is* clear that, limited though it may be in scope, it is at bottom a physiological principle. Aristotle obviously intended it to apply beyond the cases where it can receive an intelligible justification; he may have meant it to apply beyond mere physiology, but this is dubious. Certainly it fails to take account of consciousness as a factor in perception.

CHAPTER 6

418ᵃ7. Aristotle speaks here of three kinds of object of perception for each sense, which he then goes on to discuss briefly—special, common, and incidental objects. The first two are perceived in themselves or essentially (*v.* on 425ᵃ14 ff. for the supposed difficulties over common objects there). Aristotle means by this that the relation between the sense and its object is an essential one (cf. the two kinds of essential attribute specified at *Posterior Analytics* I. 4). That is to say that if we use the sense we must perceive the kind of object in question, since the sense is defined by reference to the kind of object. Or it may be the other way round instead or in addition—it may be that the definition of the object makes reference to the sense (and while it is not strictly true that, e.g., colour is defined by reference to sight, since there is, even if Aristotle does not recognize it, a difference between colour and perceived colour, it is nevertheless true that the notion of colour would be fully intelligible only to one who has sight). All this implies the existence of a common sense to which the common objects are essential, and this is asserted explicitly at 425ᵃ27. It is important to note that by 'in themselves' and 'incidentally' Aristotle does not mean 'directly' and 'indirectly', as it is often supposed. He is not here making any epistemological remarks about direct and indirect perception.

418ᵃ11. If a special object is essential to a given sense it cannot be perceived by another sense, except incidentally (cf. 425ᵃ30 ff.). Here Aristotle states the case badly. He has in mind the sort of thing that, e.g., Berkeley referred to as 'proper objects' of a sense—objects which are, so to speak, internal to the sense. It does not appear on the face of it that colour is on a par with sound and flavour in this respect. If one hears one must hear a sound, but is it necessary that if one sees one must see a colour? Only perhaps on some very broad interpretation of 'colour' which includes, for example, light and transparent objects. (For the general difficulties over the notion of proper objects of sight see G. J. Warnock, *Berkeley*, ch. 2, and W. C. Kneale in *Observation and Interpretation*, ed. Körner, pp. 151 ff.). Touch also brings with it problems. Aristotle says that it has many special objects (cf. 422ᵇ25 ff.), e.g. hot, cold, dry, wet, rough, smooth; but the plurality of objects makes it impossible for any *one* of them to be such that if we feel something by touch it must be that object, and there is nothing that they have in common except that they are tangible.

Aristotle asserts the incorrigibility of the senses with respect to their special objects in many places, e.g. 427^{b}12, 428^{a}11, 430^{b}29, *De Sensu* 442^{b}8, *Metaphysics* 1010^{b}2 ff., but at 428^{b}18 ff. he qualifies the assertion of incorrigibility by saying that error occurs as little as possible. However, he there uses as an example the perception of *white*; here he speaks of the perception of *colour* or *sound*. The point here, as the *Metaphysics* passage makes clear, is that a sense cannot confuse its object with that of another sense; it *can* err over the identity or place of the material object which possesses the quality in question. It can also presumably err over *instances* of its type of object, e.g. white vis-à-vis other colours, and it is this that 428^{b}18 ff. brings out. It is a little difficult to know exactly what is to be made of the general point that a sense cannot confuse its object with that of another sense. Aristotle uses the notion of judgement here for the first time, but applies it to the sense rather than to the animal or person (he does the latter frequently in Book III). But even if we do apply it to the person or animal, saying that a person cannot, e.g., be mistaken when using hearing as to the fact that he is hearing sound, the import of the remark is still not altogether clear. The internal connexion between a sense and its object means that the remark can only be a *conceptual* one, i.e. we cannot, logically, smell sounds. The incorrigibility that Aristotle is adducing here is in no sense a matter-of-fact incorrigibility like the incorrigibility that some philosophers have attributed to perception of so-called sense-data.

418ª16. The common objects are those which are perceptible by more than one sense (and thus they are not essential to any one special sense). They are often referred to in Aristotle's works, although the list varies somewhat (*v.* 425^{a}14 ff., *De Sensu* 437^{a}8 ff. [which says that they are perceived chiefly by sight], *De Insomniis* 458^{b}5 ff.; *De Sensu* 442^{b}5 ff. adds the rough, the smooth, the sharp, and the blunt to the list, although the first two at least are spoken of as objects of touch at *De Anima* 422^{b}26 ff. and it also says that the common objects are common at least to sight and touch; *De Memoria* 450^{a}9 ff. mentions time in connexion with the common sense although it does not specifically say that it is one of its objects). Aristotle here says that the common objects are common to, i.e. perceptible by, all the senses. This is an exaggeration; it is sight and touch which are chiefly involved and the common objects must be perceptible by these. But 425ª27 indicates that there is also a common sense to which these objects are essential (v. ad loc.).

418ª20. Physical objects, including people, are incidental objects of any sense. It does not follow, e.g., from the fact that you see something that you see a physical object; nor does the concept of a physical object involve any reference to a form of perception. The definition of a sense does not involve reference to this kind of object or vice versa. When you perceive a white man by sight the sense is affected by whiteness, and presumably the other senses are affected by other qualities of his, so that the total perception adds up to a perception of him. But this does not mean that the senses are affected by him *as such*. They are affected by him *qua* white, etc. It is noteworthy here that Aristotle turns the conceptual point about the connexion between a sense and its object into one concerned with matters of fact, i.e. one about what affects a given sense. This is typical of the whole treatment.

Lines ª22–23 are sometimes translated 'since this is incidental to the white thing which you perceive'. This is grammatically strained and I suspect that the translation is dictated by the belief that strictly speaking, according to Aristotle, one sees only the white thing, not the son of Diares. But there is no suggestion in Aristotle that it is in any way improper to speak of seeing him; it is merely that the special object of sight in this instance happens to belong to something having this identity. This is not incompatible with the point made earlier, that the senses are, strictly speaking, affected only by their special objects. It might be suggested that what Aristotle has in mind here is not this at all, but that we see a white thing which happens to be the son of Diares but that we do not see it *as* the son of Diares. In such circumstances we might afterwards speak of our having seen the son of Diares (although we did not know at the time that it was he). In this sense the son of Diares would have been the object of our perception but only incidentally. This interpretation might fit one possible translation of 425ª25–27, i.e. 'as of the son of Cleon we perceive not that he is the son of Cleon but that he is white and the white thing happened to be the son of Cleon'. But apart from the fact that the passage in question should probably be translated otherwise, this interpretation would not fit what is said at 428ᵇ20 ff., where perception of the incidental objects is said to be less subject to error than perception of the common objects. This suggestion would make no sense with regard to objects of perception which are not at the time perceived as such at all.

418ᵃ24. Aristotle implies here that the special objects are more properly objects of perception than the common objects, because in being essential to the senses they are implied by the very nature of those senses. This is misleading because it ignores the possibility, realized later, of a common sense, and even here it is suggested that the common objects are essential to something.

CHAPTER 7

418ᵃ26 ff. Aristotle now sets out to discuss sight and colour its object, together with the media necessary for the perception of colour. It is not clear whether he distinguishes colour from perceived colour (i.e. whether there can be unperceived colour). The point made in Chapter 6 about colour being essential to sight might well suggest that he does not make the distinction, if that point amounts to the claim that colour is defined by reference to sight (cf. 426ᵃ15 ff.). The visible thing which is said here to have no name appears to be phosphorescence (cf. 419ᵃ3); in what he goes on to say Aristotle appears immediately to ignore its existence except for the remark at 419ᵃ1 ff.

The transparent, whatever its nature, e.g. air or water, is the medium for sight, which colour sets in motion, light being its activity or actuality due to the agency of fire and the like. It is clear that Aristotle has little idea of the physical basis of light, as his subsequent strictures on Empedocles show. Yet it is essential for him that there must be a chain of causation between the coloured object and the eye; the transparent medium provides this. While the medium is not visible in the same way as a physical body is (we do not necessarily see the medium through which we see bodies) there is an obvious sense in which we can be said to see light. Fire brings about the actualization of the medium in the form of light just as it makes colours visible. Hence, light can be likened to colour and is said by Aristotle to be a sort of colour of the medium. What colour actually is he does not here explain. *De Sensu* 3 connects it with a limit since it is found on the surfaces of bodies, and goes so far as to explain its existence by reference to the presence of the transparent in bodies. The same thing, therefore, produces light in, for example, air, and white in bodies. Other colours are formed somehow out of white and black.

The eternal body above, mentioned at 418ᵇ9, is the aether of which the spheres which carry the heavenly bodies are made.

419ᵃ6 ff. The argument for the necessity of a medium—that if you place a coloured object on your eye you will not see it—is often adduced by Aristotle, and is generalized for all the senses, including touch, at 419ᵃ25 ff. and 423ᵇ22 ff.

CHAPTER 8

The observations which were made in the notes on the previous chapter concerning the possibility of unseen colours apply also to the possibility of unheard sounds. There are no references to unheard sounds here, and the probability is that Aristotle does not recognize their possibility (cf. 425ᵇ26 ff.). The distinction made here between actual and potential sound is one between things actually making sounds and things being able to. It is not a distinction between heard and unheard sounds.

Most of Aristotle's other remarks about hearing and sound are about the physics and physiology of these matters. They stress the part that air plays in this, as one medium and as a constituent of the sense-organ, the ear. The analogies which Aristotle notes at 420ᵃ26 ff. between tangible and audible sharpness and flatness (or bluntness) are worth noting, though by 'sharp' and 'flat' is meant in fact high and low pitch, and the Greek words are so translated elsewhere.

Aristotle turns to the special case of voice and voice-production at 420ᵇ5. He insists that, except by way of analogy, only living (ensouled) things can have a voice. At 420ᵇ27 ff. he narrows the field even further by restricting voice to things which have 'a certain imagination', on the grounds that voice is 'a particular sound which has meaning'. Imagination is required because the animal has to make a kind of movement in order to make the relevant sound and, according to Aristotle, imagination is necessary for this. (Cf. III. 10 and 11 and the accounts of the production of movement given there.) But the demand that the sounds made should have meaning seems too strict. All that is required is that the sounds should be in some sense intentional.

The biological tone of 420ᵇ14 ff. has much in common with that of III. 12 and 13. The further account of breathing mentioned is to be found at *De Respiratione*, esp. 8.

CHAPTER 9

There is little that requires comment in Aristotle's treatment of smell
(v. further *De Sensu* 5). He is right about the close connexion of smell
with taste and about the poverty of the human sense of smell. He is
right too in his observation at 421ª31 ff. that words for smells are taken
mostly from words for tastes, although his account of how it happens is
not completely clear. It appears to mean merely that the same words
are used for tastes and smells because there is a resemblance, an
analogy, between tastes and smells. It is these that he means by
'things'. Saffron, honey, etc., are mentioned merely as examples
where the resemblance of taste and smell will be evident. On the
other hand, his remark at 421ª22 ff. on the connexion between touch
and intelligence seems of very dubious validity, as is his presumably
careless remark at 421ᵇ18–19 that only men have 'the inability to
perceive without inhaling'. The structure of the argument in this
latter passage at 421ᵇ13 is not very evident, the main difficulty being
the remark about the inability to smell when something is placed on
the nostril. Aristotle appears here to be meeting a possible objection
to the closing words of the previous sentence that man cannot smell
without inhaling even when the object is placed on the nostril—the
objection that *nothing* can smell in these circumstances. With this he
agrees, but insists on the peculiarity to man of the inability to smell
without inhaling.

For the distinction made at 421ᵇ6 cf. 422ª26 ff.

CHAPTER 10

For a further treatment of taste see *De Sensu* 4.

422ª8. Aristotle rightly connects taste with touch and for this reason
asserts that it relies on the same medium—flesh, as Chapter 11 makes
clear. His argument here is not that it has no medium, but that it has
no *external* medium. Moisture, although essential to taste, is not its
medium; it acts merely as a solvent of objects, causally necessary if
those objects are to be tasted.

422ª20. Here Aristotle hints at what he makes explicit later—that
excesses of some kind in the objects of a sense make that sense in-
effective, so that the object is not perceived (cf. 424ª14, 29, 426ª30,
429ª31). His remarks on this subject at times suggest at first sight the

destruction of the *sense-organ*, but he really means, I think, only the destruction of its capacity, normally for a time only. (But 435ᵇ4 ff. perhaps suggests a different view.)

The distinction between the ways in which things are spoken of as invisible at ᵃ26 ff. is one between the simply non-visible, as sounds or smells might be said to be, and that which might be visible but is not (cf. 421ᵇ6 ff. and *v. Metaphysics* 1022ᵇ22 for a parallel distinction between kinds of *sterēsis* or privation).

422ᵇ10. Aristotle's point here is that all flavours are based on one primary opposition—the sweet and bitter—between which the other flavours lie, just as colours lie between the extremes of white and black. *De Sensu* 442ᵃ12 ff. makes clear that Aristotle thinks that the intermediate cases are formed from a mixture of the extremes in both instances.

CHAPTER 11

422ᵇ17. 'That which can perceive by touch'—literally 'that which can touch'; but this is ambiguous in English in a way that Aristotle probably did not intend. There is a similar use of the expression at 423ᵃ16 (*v.* however 434ᵇ9 ff.).

Aristotle makes explicit here the difficulty over the identification of the special object of touch which was pointed out on 418ᵃ11. He points to the fact that touch is concerned with many pairs of opposites. The apparent solution to the problem which he mentions is clearly not meant to be the real solution. The point is that opposing qualities of sound are qualities of *sound*. Of what are the hot and cold, dry and wet, rough and smooth opposing qualities?

On the other problem, of the sense-organ of touch, Aristotle is definite that it is something internal, not the flesh (cf. *De Partibus Animaliu* 656ᵃ27 ff., *De Iuventute* 469ᵃ4 ff., *De Somno* 456ᵃ1 ff. for the role of the heart as the primary sense-organ and therefore the sense-organ specially responsible for touch).

422ᵇ34. The point of the argument is to show why it is not clear to us that the flesh is not the organ of touch—the trouble being that the flesh is naturally attached to us as the media of other senses are not. This also makes it unclear to us whether touch is a single sense, since flesh is too complex (being a mixture of elements) to be *apparent* as a medium for a single sense, as air or water are. Its complexity is, however, suited to the plurality of objects that touch has. The unity of touch as a sense, despite its manifold objects, is indicated by the fact that the tongue (i.e. one single piece of flesh) can perceive all tangible objects as well as taste things. But that touch is different from taste, on the other hand, is evident from the fact that the rest of the flesh cannot taste. It cannot be said that the course of Aristotle's argument is very obvious.

As noted on 413^b4, the word αἴσθησις (*aisthēsis*) in its occurrence at 423^a6 is naturally translated as 'sensation', and it is only in connexion with touch that this is the natural translation.

423^a22 ff. Aristotle next points out that there is no real direct contact between two things which exist in air or water; so there can also be no direct contact between sense-organ and object. This does not prevent the functioning of the sense of touch any more than a membrane attached to us would do so. The only difference between the media of the distance senses and that of taste and touch is, as indicated at 423^b12, in the way in which they operate just because of the fact that the first are distance senses and the second not. He seems to imply that in the case of the distance senses perception is inevitably indirect in a way in which is it not so with touch. It is, nevertheless, unclear why this should be, on Aristotle's terms, more than a matter of degree. The illustration of the shield which Aristotle uses in this connexion at 423^b15 ff. is scarcely happy.

423^b17. Here again we have the explicit statement that perception never occurs when there is direct contact with the sense-organ (although 423^a22 ff. has made the point that real contact of this sort does not in any case occur). All the senses require media, and touch has the flesh as such (cf. 419^a6 ff.).

423^b27 ff. Aristotle now applies to touch his general formula that the object of perception makes the sense-organ 'which is potentially as it is, such as it is itself actually'. It follows that the object must be initially different from the sense-organ, and as the objects form contraries the organ must constitute a mean between them. Aristotle comes to rely on this notion more and more (cf. 424^b1, 431^a11, 19, 435^a21) and upon the connected idea that the sense constitutes a proportion (cf. 424^a25 ff., 426^a27 ff.).

Aristotle is asserting that the difference between the sense-organ and the object is the basis of the discrimination of objects, e.g. to perceive hotness the organ must be sufficiently cold. (How this applies to the organs of senses like sight it is impossible to see.) The transition from this to the idea that the sense is itself a mean and that the mean is 'capable of judging' is obscure; for it is the *sense-organ* which must constitute the mean if anything does; its state is the mean state. Hence, by 'sense' Aristotle must mean the sense-organ here, and it is in terms of this that the doctrine must be interpreted.

For the destructive nature of what is in excess see on 422ᵃ20.

CHAPTER 12

424ᵃ17. Here Aristotle produces another formula to sum up sense-perception—that it consists in receiving the form of the object without its matter. In this passage he says that it is the sense which does this, but later passages at 425ᵇ23 and 435ᵃ22 reveal that it is really the sense-organ that does so. In fact, as he says here, a sense is merely a potentiality possessed by a sense-organ and it can in consequence be affected only if and as the sense-organ is. As in the case of the other formula which he introduced at 418ᵃ3 (i.e. that that which can perceive is potentially such as the object of perception is actually), the range of applicability of the present formula seems limited and it fits touch best. It is not easy to see how the eye can receive colour when we see, or the ear sound when we hear.

Aristotle goes on to 'explain' the reception of form in terms of the affection of a sense by things in virtue of their form, i.e. in perception the sense is affected by an object just in so far as it is of the relevant form and not because it is what it is. For example, when we see a man, the sense of sight is affected by him in so far as he is, say, white, and not because he is a rational, non-feathered biped. Hence it is only in respect of the relevant aspect of a thing that a sense can be affected by it. To the extent that this is clear at all, it is not evident how it works for every case of sense-perception; since a sense can be affected only in so far as the sense-organ is, the limitations referred to above apply. The trouble is that Aristotle tries to invoke a causal theory of perception in order to explain the essential connexion between a sense and its object which was set out in Chapter 6. This is impossible, since the issues involved are quite different.

The connexion between a sense and its organ which is referred to above is dealt with by a formula which is used frequently hereafter (cf. 425ᵇ27, 426ᵃ16, 427ᵃ3, 431ᵃ14, 19, 432ᵇ1)—they are the same, but different in εἶναι (*einai*). This is to say that they are numerically one, but different in essence or function. The sense-organ is an extended thing but the sense is a potentiality or capacity of that thing. There are not two things but one organ which can be viewed either from the point of view of its physical nature or from the point of view of its function. (I take it that τὸ εἶναι is in fact short for e.g. τὸ αἰσθητηρίῳ εἶναι, i.e. what it is for it to be a sense-organ—as I have translated similar phrases elsewhere. Thus it denotes the essence of the thing.)

424ᵃ28. For the destruction of a sense by excesses in its objects see on 422ᵃ20. Aristotle says here that it is the sense-organ which is destroyed, but, as he goes on to indicate, only in respect of its capacity or form as a sense. In other words, excess prevents the proper functioning of the sense-organ.

I do not think that, when Aristotle speaks of the consonance of the strings of an instrument being destroyed by too violent a blow, the reference to consonance implies anything to do with the harmony of different strings. It is the consonance and pitch of a single string which is destroyed when it is struck too violently; the string does not then sound properly at the right pitch and with the proper timbre. (Cf. 426ᵃ27, 29, and ᵇ6 for similar uses of συμφωνία [*sumphōnia*] applied to voice. 426ᵇ6 seems to suggest that Aristotle considers any single tone of this kind to be a blend of higher and lower tones which in this way forms a new tone; cf. *De Sensu* 447ᵃ29 ff., especially 447ᵇ2 with its suggestion that any mixture of tones must be heard as a new tone. See also *De Sensu* 439ᵇ19 ff. where Aristotle draws an analogy between colours as mixtures and consonances [*sumphōniai*]. The latter must therefore be tones of definite pitch which arise from mixture of the high and low; cf. *Metaphysics* 1043ᵃ10.) The analogy between the effect on the sense and on a string of excessive stimulation indicates the direction in which the word λόγος (*logos*) (here translated 'principle') is being taken, so as to cover the notions of proportion or mean. This is made explicit in the reference to the mean which follows and is also brought out at 426ᵃ27 ff.

Plants do not perceive although they are affected by tangible objects. Aristotle's explanation is that they do not have a mean (i.e. a sense as specified at 424ᵃ27 ff.), so as to be affected in the right way. He provides little else in the way of explanation, but the closing words are supposed to add to what has been said. But how are plants affected by the matter as well? Presumably they take in some kind of matter (e.g. moisture) when warmed. But is this not also true of the warming of a sense-organ? If not, how is the reception of the form (the heat) without the matter to be interpreted, unless Aristotle means that the sense-organ becomes warm without taking in any hot matter? But how does this come about? Aristotle's account of sense-perception remains in this respect mysterious.

424ᵇ3. This passage consists of a series of questions, objections, and counter-objections. Aristotle first denies that anything which cannot perceive can be affected by an object of perception. He then produces another argument for this conclusion: objects of sight, hearing, and smell do not affect bodies. But tangible objects and flavours do. For bodies must be affected by something. (It is possible to see what he is getting at when he speaks of tangible objects—they include the hot and the cold; but it is difficult to see the relevance of flavours, unless he is here refusing to make the distinction between the quality and the thing which it is in.) Given that tangible objects and flavours affect bodies, why do not other objects of perception do so? Or is there a limitation in the number and kind of things which can be so affected?

It is not clear what is supposed to emerge from this, except that at the end Aristotle makes a hypothetical distinction between one case of perception and being affected, to the effect that being affected, while a necessary condition of perception, is not sufficient. The whole passage looks like a number of lecturer's questions thrown out seriatim by way of challenge. Aristotle's position is not, however, really in doubt.

BOOK III

CHAPTER 1

424ᵇ22. The argument presented at the beginning of this chapter is both obscure in itself and obscurely set out. This is perhaps inevitable in any argument which seeks to prove something that seems to be a matter of empirical fact—the number of the senses that animals and human beings have. It is difficult to make much of the argument taken as a whole. It seems, in a reconstructed form, to run as follows:

(*a*) The senses function either by contact or through media.
(*b*) Wherever there is a sense there is a sense-organ.

(c) We do have touch and thereby perception of anything which is perceptible by contact. There remains the other alternative mentioned under (a)—perception through media.

(d) Perception through media is perception by means of one or other of the elements, of which there are four—earth, fire, air, and water.

(e) If there is perception through a medium, the sense-organ must be akin to the medium. This might be possible in two ways:

   (i) If two things different in kind are perceived through one medium alone, they must be perceptible by a sense-organ of the same kind.

   (ii) If two things different in kind are perceived through more than one medium, then they may be perceptible by sense-organs of one or other of these kinds.

(f) The sense-organs for the senses using media are composed of air or water only; and some animals have one or other (or both?) of these. (Aristotle does not say what presumably needs saying—(1) that (e) (i) above does not occur, i.e. that no distance sense depends in all animals on the same one medium, and (2) that the only two media available under (e) (ii) are water and air.)

(g) Hence, there are no other sense-organs (or senses) than those which exist, unless there are any further elements than those which exist now.

Apart from the points noted under (f), Aristotle does not justify (d) and (e), especially the point that there must be a kinship between the sense-organ and the medium. But the main feature is that (c) and (f) seem to be based on empirical facts or supposed empirical facts, so that the validity of the conclusion in the end depends on just this. All that the argument could be taken to show, if it were valid, is that we have touch, taste (the other contact sense), and the distance senses which depend on water and air as media (i.e. according to Aristotle, sight, hearing, and smell). But might there not be senses depending on other media, e.g. fire or some other element apart from the four canonical ones? In effect, Aristotle admits the latter possibility, but his rejection of the former depends purely on what he takes the empirical facts to be. (In any case, he differs in his view of them from what he says elsewhere, e.g. at *De Sensu* 438ᵇ16 ff., where he associates smell with fire on the grounds that its object is smoky vapour and that the sense-organ must therefore be potentially hot; it is so, he says, because being near the brain [the cooling system of the body] it is cold and therefore potentially hot. See on 418^{a}3.)

It is customary in modern textbooks of psychology to say that there are far more senses than the traditional five (e.g. kinaesthesis, somaesthesis). It is not clear what Aristotle would have said about this; he might have classified the additional senses under contact senses. The view that there are three distance senses would still be valid. But that there are these three alone remains at best a matter of empirical fact. Aristotle's argument cannot rule out the *possibility* of other senses. But, as the last sentence of the passage indicates, it may be the case that it was not intended to, even if the grounds adduced for not excluding other possibilities altogether are suspect. If this is so, it is not clear why Aristotle resorts to all the paraphernalia of the argument here presented.

425^{a}14. It has sometimes been suggested that there is a conflict between the 'incidentally' which occurs at the beginning of this passage at ^{a}15 and the 'not incidentally' which occurs towards the end at ^{a}28. There is in fact no such conflict. Aristotle is here denying that there is a *special sense-organ* for perception of the common objects mentioned earlier in II. 6, and hence he denies also that there is a *special sense* for them. This is compatible with the assertion at ^{a}27–28 that there is a common sense for them and that they are essential to this (*v.* on 418^{a}7 for this notion); it is also compatible with the notion that we perceive the common objects through the sense-organs for the special senses, and hence by those senses (*v.* on 418^{a}16). But since the common objects are perceptible by more than one special sense they are not essential to any one of them. Hence Aristotle says that we perceive them by each sense incidentally (sc. by each special sense incidentally), and that there is no special sense for them. 425^{a}27 says that there is in fact a common sense, i.e. a sense shared by different sense-organs and one to which the common objects are essential. The reason why there must be such a sense is that the common objects are not assimilable to any of the objects which are merely incidental objects of perception. They are like the special objects in status except that they are perceived by more than one special sense; they are objects essential to a form of perception (a point which might be put in more modern terms by saying that the notion of, e.g., shape is ultimately intelligible only to one who has perception, and perception via more than one sense, so that the criteria of shape, etc., are both visual and tactual—cf. my *Seeing Things as They Are*, pp. 12 ff.).

Aristotle explains the ways in which movement plays a role in the perception of the common objects. The passage has sometimes been suspected as a gloss, but there is nothing fundamentally wrong with it. The movement required for perception of magnitude might be either physical or mental, and that required for perception of number as a negation of continuity is most plausibly to be interpreted as a mental one. It would not be unlike Aristotle to run physical movement together with mental movement, i.e. changes of attention (cf. *Physics* 263ª25 ff., where counting is put on the same level as physical movement). Number is also said to be perceived through the special objects; the point is presumably that each sense perceives one thing at a time and hence we perceive the object as one—so unity. A plurality of the senses or a plurality of occasions on which the sense is exercised gives perception of plurality or number.

Having given an account of the perception of the common objects, Aristotle goes on to explain how this differentiates it from forms of incidental perception. If there *were* a special sense for, e.g., movement, how should we perceive movement also by sight, as we undoubtedly do? Would it not be like seeing the sweetness of something, i.e. using one sense to perceive the objects essential to another? The explanation of the latter phenomenon which follows *may* be the same as that given at 425ª30 ff.—that the senses perceive each other's objects incidentally in joint perception. But this is not a necessary interpretation of 425ª21–24, which can be interpreted as saying that because we have perceived sweetness and whiteness falling together in, e.g., sugar, it happens that when we see sugar again (whiteness and sweetness falling together) we immediately see it as sweet. In that case the words 'at the same time' would go with 'recognize' and there would be no necessary implication of simultaneous perception of objects of different senses. (*De Sensu* 7 brings forward a whole series of objections against the possibility of such simultaneous perception of different objects, although it ends with an apparent recognition and explanation of the fact that this is possible in some cases, because of 'that which can perceive all things' [τὸ αἰσθητικὸν πάντων—*to aisthētikon pantōn*], the general and unified faculty of perception of which the individual senses are mere manifestations. See further on 425ª30.) Commentators usually object to the notion of seeing that something is sweet, but there can be no valid objection to speaking in this way; the objection presumably stems from the prejudice that there must be an intrinsic connexion between sight and its objects if we are to speak of seeing at all.

The phenomenon in question is no doubt a product of learning or experience, but this does not make it any the less a case of seeing.

The final possibility that Aristotle mentions (in the sentence given in brackets) is incidental perception in the strictest sense. The phenomenon which has been discussed above is at the most the incidental perception by one sense of the essential objects of another. The phenomenon which he now mentions is the perception of objects which are not essential to *any* sense, i.e. an identifiable person or physical object (v. on 418ᵃ20). When we see the son of Cleon we do so because we see a white thing which happens to be the son of Cleon. On an alternative and perhaps more usual translation of the passage, i.e. 'as of the son of Cleon we perceive not that he is the son of Cleon but that he is white, and the white object happens to be the son of Cleon', it might be thought, as was suggested on 418ᵃ20, that Aristotle is describing a case in which we perceive a white thing without perceiving it *as* the son of Cleon, and that we perceive the son of Cleon incidentally in this sense, without knowing that it is he. Against this it has to be said that such an interpretation would not be at all plausible as providing a possible account of perception of the common objects, which is what Aristotle is attempting to do. For surely any account of this must be an account of the perception of the common objects *as* such. It could not be the case that, if we did not perceive the common objects essentially by the common sense, the only alternatives would be that we should perceive them either as we perceive the sweet by sight or as we perceive the son of Cleon without being aware that it is he. In fact Aristotle never takes into consideration cases like the last; he always has in mind cases of perceiving *X* as *X*. The translation and interpretation which I have offered is more in line with 418ᵃ20 ff. (and is one which Hicks recommends in his commentary although he does not adopt it in the translation).

Aristotle states finally that perception of the common objects is like none of the preceding and asserts categorically that they are essential objects of a common sense, i.e. a potentiality for perceiving objects which are perceptible by more than one special sense-organ and which are thus common to those sense-organs. (The words αἴσθησιν κοινήν [aisthēsin koinēn], which occur in Aristotle only here and at *De Memoria* 450ᵃ10 and *De Partibus Animalium* 686ᵃ27 ff., must be translated 'common sense' despite the lack of a definite article. Suggestions like 'general sensibility' which have sometimes been made do not fit the point which Aristotle is making, especially the point that the objects are not incidental. For what could it mean to speak of the common objects being 'not incidental' to a general sensibility?)

425ᵃ30. Aristotle now discusses another kind of incidental perception (which may or may not be different from that discussed in the previous section at 425ᵃ21 ff., i.e. seeing the sweetness of something). This results from joint or simultaneous perception by more than one sense. As already noted on the previous section, *De Sensu* 7 raises difficulties about this whole notion but eventually seems to allow some cases of it because of the existence of the general and unified faculty of perception ('that which can perceive all things'). *De Somno* 455ᵃ16 refers to the existence of a common potentiality (κοινὴ δύναμις—*koinē dunamis*) for analogous reasons. The idea which is introduced here of the senses forming a unity also underlies much of the discussion in III. 2 and is finally illustrated by the analogy of a point at 427ᵃ10. It is only because the senses form a unity and because the object is one that it is possible to speak of one sense perceiving the objects of another incidentally. Aristotle adds that this very fact may give rise to mistakes of identity, for obvious reasons.

The sentence in brackets might conceivably be translated 'it is not the task of either {sense} at any rate to say that both are one', implying that the recognition of the unity of the objects must come from the unity of the senses. (It is indeed suggested by Hicks in his commentary that this implies a reference to the common sense, but this is a mistake; the notions of a unity of the senses and of a common sense are quite different, and even if the common sense was invoked earlier at 425ᵃ16 for perception of unity, this was not as a piece of psychological machinery as would be implied here.) On the other hand, the noun to go with ἑτέρας (*heteras*) (translated as 'either' above and as 'further' in my translation) has to be supplied, and it is presumably the αἴσθησις (*aisthēsis*) of the previous line. This must be translated as 'perception' not as 'sense'. It might still be possible to interpret the sentence as saying that it is not the task of either perception by itself to say that the objects are one, implying the necessity for joint perception. But since only one perception has been mentioned, I am inclined to think that is is better to interpret the sentence as I have done—'it is not the task of any further perception . . .', implying the sufficiency of joint perception. That is to say that we do not, e.g., perceive yellowness and bitterness and *then* that they are together.

425ᵇ4. The question posed here looks at first sight as if it were a quite general question about the reasons for a plurality of senses. But if this is in fact the case, it has to be pointed out that there are much more obvious reasons of a teleological kind for a plurality of senses, e.g. in order that we may see as well as hear. It is possible, therefore, that Aristotle is asking merely why we have a plurality of senses for the common objects, although if this is so it must be confessed that the passage reads awkwardly.

Is Aristotle right in pointing out that in the extreme hypothetical case quoted the common objects would not be apparent? It may indeed seem almost analytic that it would be so; but this is not in fact the case, since it is presumably of the special senses that he is supposing that sight might be the sole example, and there might be a common sense as well. Although in these circumstances we should hardly *call* that sense 'common', this would not rule out the capacity for perceiving the objects which *are* common as things are now. In that case it is not clear why the common objects should be more apparent with a plurality of senses, any more than colour needs a plurality of senses to be apparent. What the plurality of senses makes clear is that the common objects are *common*, not that they exist. Aristotle appears to give way to the temptation, already noted under 418ᵃ24, to suppose that the special objects are somehow more fundamentally objects of perception. It is to be noted that the common objects are said to accompany the special objects, and more particularly that colour and magnitude are said to accompany each other invariably, i.e. that everything that is coloured is also extended and vice versa.

CHAPTER 2

This chapter is a rambling one, but it begins and ends with a consideration of what are fundamentally the problems of self-consciousness.

425ᵇ12. Aristotle starts off his discussion of the problem how we know that we perceive with the assertion, which he never justifies, that we perceive that we perceive. The problem is how this is possible. Here he eliminates the possibility that we know that we see by means of a different sense. This would mean that the object of sight, colour, would be an object of this sense too, which goes against the whole notion of an object of a sense. (Aristotle actually speaks of colour as the *subject* of sight, because as its object it is what the sense judges about; cf. 426ᵇ8.) It is not clear why Aristotle supposes the consequence to follow. He seems to assume that if I perceive by sense *Y* that I see

X, I must therefore perceive *X* by *Y*. It is of course possible to use the words 'I see that I am tasting a strawberry' in such a way that it follows that I see a strawberry; but this is because the words are tantamount to 'I see that it is a strawberry that I am tasting'. One's knowledge that one was tasting a strawberry would then be something additional. On the other hand, one can clearly be aware that one is seeing without being aware of what one is seeing. This awareness is not of course awareness by another sense; but then it is impossible to know what would be the case in impossible circumstances, and what Aristotle is considering *is* impossible. In other words the solution to the problem which Aristotle is attacking is impossible, but not for his reasons.

425ᵇ15. The second objection is better—that the supposition would generate an infinite regress. Leibniz uses a similar argument in connexion with 'apperception'.

425ᵇ17. Aristotle now raises a difficulty over the thesis that it is by sight that we perceive that we see, a difficulty which he resolves in the end simply by saying that perception by sight is not a single thing. (Cf. *De Somno* 455ª16 ff. with its assertion that it is not by sight that one sees [*sic*] that one sees, but by the common potentiality which is common to all the senses.) It is doubtful, however, whether the consideration that he brings to bear on the question, i.e. that perception by sight is not a single thing, is necessarily relevant to his problem; perception by sight might be multifarious, as he indicates by the case of judging darkness and light, but not necessarily in the right respect. What is needed here is the concept of self-consciousness, itself involving the notion of a subject or person who perceives and is aware of doing so. Such notions, along with that of personal identity, are completely missing from Aristotle's philosophy of mind, as noted in the Introduction.

The difficulty that he brings forward (according to the text adopted) is that if seeing is seeing colour or what is coloured, and if one is to see that which sees, this will be coloured. But he goes on later to admit that that which sees (i.e. the organ of vision) is in a way coloured—an admission which undermines his argument. This argument is, however, irrelevant in any case, since his concern should be with seeing *that* one sees, and he should show that this involves seeing the thing which sees; this he fails to do.

(The textual crux referred to above is whether in the three occurrences of the phrase at ª19 and ª22 one should read τὸ ὁρῶν [*to horon*—

that which sees] or τὸ ὁρᾶν [to horan—seeing]. It is clear that in the last of these we should read τὸ ὁρῶν, because the phrase refers to the sense-organ, as the following remarks make clear. This means that at the second occurrence in ^{a}19 we should read τὸ ὁρῶν also, or else the remark at ^{a}22 would be pointless. It remains a question whether in the first occurrence we may read τὸ ὁρᾶν, which if scarcely grammatical might seem more to the point in the context—'if one is to see seeing'. The snag is that in that case it is not at all clear why it should follow that 'that which sees primarily will have colour'. There seems no way of making the argument coherent.)

The passage ends with a repetition of the formula for sense-perception given earlier at 424^{a}17; on this occasion the fact that it has to do with the sense-organ is made explicit. It is also used to account for after-images and perhaps other images. It also leads on to some general considerations about the relation between the senses and their objects.

425^{b}26. For the formula used in the first sentence of this passage see on 424^{a}17. Aristotle means here that the actual sounding of an object and actual hearing are coincident, in the sense that only one movement or change takes place but this can be regarded from two points of view, either as hearing a sound or as something sounding (cf. *Physics* 202^{a}18 ff. for a similar treatment of uphill and downhill and an application of this to change). This implies that actual sounding cannot take place without actual hearing and vice versa. It is tempting to suppose that what Aristotle is referring to is the fact that sound can be viewed as the internal object of hearing, i.e. that one cannot hear without there being a sound to hear; but this relationship does not hold good vice versa, and Aristotle clearly wishes the connexion to hold in both directions. It is rather that he supposes that there is one single movement or change going on, which can be considered as hearing from the point of view of the subject, sounding from the point of view of the object. The exact nature of this change is left obscure, but Aristotle's account is unsatisfactory in any case, because he is satisfied with what is a purely physical account of the matter and this fails to take note of the fact that hearing is a 'modification of consciousness' of which sound is the appropriate object; 'hearing' is not merely a name for a kind of physical change. This difficulty runs right through Aristotle's account of perception. It remains true that we should not have a concept of sounding if we did not have one of hearing, and perhaps, though in a somewhat different way, vice versa; but this conceptual connexion does not amount to the thesis 'no actual sounding without actual hearing'. Indeed this thesis is manifestly false, since there are many sounds actually occurring that no one hears. A sound is rather a possible object of hearing.

I have translated the activity of hearing as 'listening'. This is perhaps not quite right as listening implies attention. But no other suitable word really exists.

426ᵃ2. The change or movement which can be viewed either as the activity of the sense-organ or as that of the object is now said to be in the sense-organ, i.e. that which is potentially hearing. With the assumption that perception is a form of change or of being affected, this is in conformity with Aristotle's general dictum that change or movement takes place in that which is moved (cf. 414ᵃ4 ff. and *Physics* 202ᵃ13 ff.). It follows from this that there can (indeed must) be an unmoved mover, as is hinted at ᵃ5–6 in the remark that it is not necessary 'for that which produces movement to be itself moved'.

426ᵃ8. Aristotle now generalizes his account from hearing to the other senses, while pointing out that some of the forms of activity in question have no name, e.g. the activity of colour or flavour. He seems to attach no importance to this fact, but it perhaps serves as an indication that there are differences between hearing and sight and perhaps between these and some of the other senses. The fact that there is no word for the 'activity' of colour and taste, while there is one for that of sound, may have something to do with the fact that sounds are emitted from objects and can persist to some extent like smells in the absence of their source (just because of the features of the causal processes involved). Sounds and smells are produced in a way in which colours and tastes are not. (It has to be admitted that light from very distant objects, like stars, may be perceptible when its source no longer exists; but this is an exceptional case, not the norm, and as a result we think of colours as belonging to bodies in a way in which sounds do not generally belong.)

426ᵃ15. Aristotle here uses the point which he has made in order to criticize a form of subjective idealism attributable at any rate to Protagoras and perhaps to others. His formula commits him to the view that there cannot be actual hearing without actual sounding and vice versa, and so also for the other senses. This he now puts forward as the truth of the matter. The earlier thinkers had not made sufficient distinctions. Their view does not apply to, e.g., potential sounding and hearing. If the slogan of the earlier philosophers referred to is taken at its face value, it may seem that the situation should really be the other way round. There can be actual sounds without actual hearing, but not potential sounds without potential hearing—and similarly for the other senses in so far as the potential/actual distinction can be made. For there can be sounds without anyone hearing them, while if it is possible for a sound to be made by something, it must also be possible for it to be heard. But, as noted on II. 7 and 8, Aristotle does not really distinguish between sounds and perceived sounds, colours and perceived colours, etc. It is of course true that there cannot be an actually perceived sound without someone actually perceiving it, while the potentiality to perceive sound might exist without there existing any potentiality to produce perceptible sounds. Hence, in this sense, Aristotle's comment may be considered valid.

426ª27. For 'consonance' see the note on 424ª28 ff.

The MSS. here read 'If consonance is a kind of voice . . .', but on this reading the argument would be invalid, and it is not clear in any case why 'consonance' should be a kind of voice rather than a kind of sound. The objection to the reading here adopted is usually put by saying that not all voice is a kind of consonance, if by 'consonance' is meant 'concord'. But as stated on 424ª28 ff., it is probable that it means nothing of the kind, but a blend of high- and low-pitched sounds. Aristotle seems here, as at *De Sensu* 439ᵇ19 ff. and 447ª29 ff. and elsewhere, to think of sounds, like colours, as blends of extremes. Given the reading adopted, his point here is that voice consists of pitched sound and this is a blend of high and low sounds in a proportion. Since, as he has claimed earlier, the activity of hearing and sound are one and the same, hearing can similarly be spoken of as a proportion, i.e. a proportionate blend between extremes presumably in the processes of the ear. It might be argued that not all sounds are pitched in this way as voice is, but Aristotle might reply by saying that hearing functions properly in respect of pitched sounds and that when the sound has uncertain and indefinite pitch there is similar indefiniteness and uncertainty in hearing. (There might indeed be something to this claim.) Moreover, as he goes on to say, extremities of pitch make the functioning of the sense impossible. For this notion of the destruction of the sense see on 422ª20 ff.

At 426ᵇ4 Aristotle uses the word 'proportion' (λόγος—*logos*) of the sense itself in view of what is said above. ·Aristotle's point about pleasure is that while unmixed objects can cause pleasure when perceived, it is the mixed objects which cause most pleasure just because the sense itself is in a way a mixture or proportion. When the sense is concerned with things which consist of proportionate mixtures it functions properly, as indicated above. Hence the pleasure.

426ᵇ8. For 'subject' see on 425ᵇ12 ff.

By 'judges' here Aristotle means 'discriminates'. Indeed the translation would have read better with the substitution of that word. But Aristotle speaks of judgement where discrimination is not obviously so appropriate, and in the interests of consistency I have kept the more general, but also on occasion more awkward, word 'judge'.

Aristotle here turns back from a consideration of the senses and their objects to the more general problems concerned with self-consciousness. The specific problem introduced here is how discrimination between objects of different senses is possible (cf. *De Sensu* 7 and *De Somno* 455ª17 ff.). Aristotle assumes, as he does in discussing the problem how we are aware that we perceive, that the awareness which is involved is a perceptual awareness, or, to be more exact, since he does not speak of awareness, that the discrimination is perceptual—made possible by a unity of the senses (*v*. on 425ᵇ17 for Aristotle's failure to produce a proper analysis of self-consciousness).

The last sentence of the passage presents the problem: what is it of which Aristotle says that flesh is not the ultimate sense-organ? It has been suggested (*a*) that it is touch (Ross; cf. 423ᵇ20 ff.), and (*b*) that it is the common sense (Hicks). Both of these suggestions must be rejected on the ground that they do not connect Aristotle's point with what he has said about discrimination between objects of different senses, although Ross's suggestion is the nearer to the truth. The point is that we do not always discriminate objects when the flesh is touched (e.g. when the eye is touched we cannot discriminate an object of vision from that of touch). But we ought to do so if flesh (of which the eye is made up) were the ultimate sense-organ. That is to say that flesh cannot be the ultimate sense-organ for all perception including the perception that what we are feeling is not an object of vision. According to the *Parva Naturalia* (*De Iuventute* 4, *De Somno* 2) it is the heart which is the ultimate organ which is responsible for sense-perception as for other forms of life.

426ᵇ17. Aristotle now argues that one could not discriminate the object of one sense from that of another if the senses were not connected. Otherwise it would be just like two quite different people judging—in which case it could not be immediately evident to either separately that they were concerned with different things. Hence there must be a unity to the senses—they must constitute one thing.

426ᵇ23. Aristotle adds that the judgements involved in the discrimination must be simultaneous and directed to simultaneous and contemporaneous occurrences. This is the point of the words 'it so asserts both now and that they are different now'. Discrimination is something done by a person at a single time with reference to what is taking place at that same time.

426ᵇ29. Aristotle now brings forward objections to the position so far arrived at (cf. *De Sensu* 7 for similar and more detailed objections):

(a) The same thing cannot be moved at the same time in opposite ways.

(b) Perception and thought, as forms of being affected, involve being moved; the motions in question may be opposed or just different.

(c) Perhaps the subject which discriminates is numerically one but differentiated in function (cf. on 424ᵃ17 for this notion). *But*, while the same thing can be both of a pair of opposites, as it must be if it is to be so affected, it cannot be so actually at the same time. So one cannot perceive or think both of a pair of opposites simultaneously, if perception and thought are of this kind, i.e. cases of being affected.

It might be thought that this would not be an objection to the same thing being moved at the same time in ways which are different without being opposed; but the passage at 431ᵃ19 and 20 ff., which seems to assert very categorically the singleness of sense, seems also to argue that it makes no difference whether the objects concerned are opposed or just different. *De Sensu* 449ᵃ3 ff., on the other hand, seems to allow that there may be simultaneous perception of things different in kind or genus at least, and it is difficulties over simultaneous perception of different objects which underlie the objections brought forward here in the *De Anima*. These objections depend, of course, on the idea that perceiving something is being affected or moved by it. It may be that the next section with its emphasis on judgement is meant to undermine that idea, but if so Aristotle does not make the point really clear. Another point is that neither here nor in *De Sensu* 7 does Aristotle pay any attention to the fact that the objects of perception may occupy a *field*—something obvious in the case of the field of vision, even if the existence of a field of this kind is problematic in the case of the other senses.

427ª9. Aristotle claims here to give the final solution to his problem. That which judges or discriminates, the unified sense (presumably the αἰσθητικὸν πάντων [*aisthētikon pantōn*]—that which can perceive all things—of *De Sensu* 449ª18 and the κοινὴ δύναμις [*koinē dunamis*]—the common potentiality—of *De Somno* 455ª16), is like a point. This is a single thing but *qua* forming a boundary between two sections of a line it can be treated as the starting-point of two lines, and hence as itself two. So far this is a mere analogy to illustrate the notion of being numerically one but divided in function. Aristotle goes on to speak of that which judges or discriminates *using* the point twice. The subject seems here to have become the person or animal, and this uses the single faculty twice, once to attend to, e.g., white and to discriminate it from, e.g., sweet, and secondly to attend to sweet and discriminate it from white. Whether Aristotle is conscious of what is implied here— the notion of a person with a unity of consciousness—and whether the emphasis on judgement in perception is meant to provide a contrast with the previous emphasis on perception as a form of being affected is not clear. But the real emphasis is apparently laid upon the analogy of a point—an analogy which is not perspicuous in its implications, to say the least.

There is no explicit reference to the common sense anywhere in this chapter, nor would such a reference be in place. The unified faculty of sense which is invoked here and in the *Parva Naturalia* is one the exercise of which is carried out through any or all of the senses and is therefore common to all. The common sense is not common in this way, but because it is exercised by more than one sense-organ and with reference to objects which are perceptible through more than one sense. The fact that certain objects are perceptible through different senses implies that those senses form a unity *only* in that they have these objects in common, and in no other way (cf. the situation in which the same object is seen and thought of; this would not imply the unity of sight and thought, even if there is the presupposition that it is the same person who sees and thinks of the object). On the other hand, the possibility of discriminating between objects of different senses does imply a kind of unity of the senses; it presupposes, moreover, a form of self-consciousness, as perception of the common objects does not. The common sense is thus rightly invoked by Aristotle only with reference to the perception of the common objects, and none of the problems dealt with in this chapter have anything to do with this notion. They are concerned with self-consciousness and the unity of the senses (cf. Kant's synthetic unity of apperception). These are quite different ideas. Hence neither this chapter nor the parallel discussions in the *Parva Naturalia* referred to above have anything to do with the common sense.

CHAPTER 3

This chapter is mainly about imagination, which Aristotle says at 428ª1 is primarily 'that in virtue of which we say that an image occurs to us'. Despite this definition, the chapter covers much more than imagination in our sense; it is about *phantasia* (φαντασία) and as such covers appearances in general. This gives the chapter a disjointed look, its principle of unity being a loose one. It does, however, provide a transition from perception to thinking in general.

427ª17. Aristotle begins to differentiate perception from thinking. Despite his comments on his predecessors (e.g. Parmenides, Empedocles, and Democritus), who tended to assimilate perception to thinking, assuming that they were both forms of like being affected by like and treating them both from a physical point of view, Aristotle's own accounts of perception and thought are remarkably parallel. They both involve the assimilation of the faculty to its object, the reception of form without matter, incorrigibility in relation to certain objects, and a reliance upon judgement. The only difference is that since the intellect has no specific organ the first two of these notions cannot be interpreted, as in the case of sense-perception, in terms of an organ, as a physical or physiological doctrine. Aristotle's positive account of the intellect is to be found in the next chapter.

Aristotle uses here a great variety of terms to deal with different aspects of thinking, belief, etc. Despite some indications to the contrary, there is probably little to be made in the way of a distinction between *to phronein* (τὸ φρονεῖν) and *to noein* (τὸ νοεῖν), which have been translated 'understanding' and 'thinking' respectively. It may be that '*to phronein*' suggests more of an awareness of an object, but if so Aristotle makes little of the difference. There seems to be hardly any connexion between the use of '*to phronein*' here and the use of '*phronēsis*' (φρόνησις) in the *Nicomachean Ethics* to refer to practical reason. It is to be noted too that later in this chapter Aristotle includes knowledge, belief, etc. under thinking.

Aristotle's objection to his predecessors that they failed to take account of error seems valid, since no purely physical account could deal with this. The suggestion that error consists of contact with the unlike is obviously puerile, and Aristotle rightly rejects it hotly. His remark that error and knowledge seem to be the same in respect of the opposites probably means that they have the same object not an opposite one as the rejected account might suggest.

The second reason adduced for distinguishing perception and thinking—that false or incorrect thinking is possible—is a bad one, since it is only of the special objects that perception has been said to be always true. In any case 428ᵇ19 casts doubt even on this, while 430ª26 ff. distinguishes a form of *thinking* which is always true. The other reason offered, that thinking is found in some animals only, i.e. those which have reason, is better. The significance of the last few words of the section is that they are presumably meant to meet a hypothetical objection that imagination *is* found in all animals (on which contrast 428ª8 ff., 428ª16 ff., and 434ª5 ff.), and that imagination is a form of thinking. Aristotle's reply is that it is not so in the proper sense; it is dependent on perception.

The word ὑπόληψις (*hupolēpsis*) has been translated 'supposal'. It is a difficult word to translate since it appears to express a very general notion which functions somewhat as the notion of judgement did in the writings of the Absolute Idealists such as Bradley. 427ᵇ24 ff. indicates that it covers what would be, to us, very different things.

427ᵇ16. The interpretation of the opening words of this section which is accepted in the translation is due ultimately to Freudenthal. It might be argued that the natural translation of the words if νόησις (*noēsis*) is retained would be 'that thinking and supposal are not the same . . .'. But in that case, since the passage goes on to talk about imagination, it would be necessary to interpret 'thinking' as covering imagination, and this is awkward in view of the preceding differentiation between imagination and thinking (*dianoia*—διάνοια). Ross in the O.C.T. proposes to delete the offending word. Whatever be the textual solution the sense required is clear enough.

Aristotle's way of distinguishing between imagining and supposing seems to imply that the latter cannot be subject to the will. We cannot believe what we want to; there have to be taken into account the facts or our view of them. It is not absolutely clear that this is correct, since we can at any rate set out to believe things or make ourselves believe things. On the other hand, truth and falsity are certainly essential characteristics of belief, while they are not pertinent to imagination in the same way. The real point is that beliefs are determined at least by *our view of the facts*; this is not true of imagining something.

What Aristotle says in the latter half of the passage seems quite correct.

427ᵇ24. The wideness of the notion of supposal has been noted above on 427ᵃ17 ff.

427ᵇ27. *Thought* here receives a very general sense so as to cover both imagination and epistemic notions like those of belief and knowledge (given what is said about supposal in the previous section).

It has been plausibly suggested that the metaphorical sense of the term 'imagination' is that which connects it with appearances rather than images (φαίνεσθαι—*phainesthai* rather than φαντάζεσθαι—*phantazesthai*). But in the sequel Aristotle makes many references to 'appearing' under the heading of imagination proper; there is clearly little consistency here.

428ᵃ5. Aristotle brings five considerations to bear against the identification of imagination and perception. As he expresses the points only the last has any cogency; the first three seem invalid or problematical as they stand, while the fourth is concerned with imagination in the sense of appearances only and as these are perceptual phenomena they do not serve to mark a distinction from perception. The last consideration at least indicates that there may be images when there is no perception.

1. Imagination functions in dreams when perception is not present either potentially or actually. (But is not perception present potentially in sleep, even if not in quite the same way as with a man who is awake but has his eyes closed?)

2. Perception is always present but not imagination. (The next sentence makes clear that this means 'present in all animals'. The difficulty over ants and bees has been pointed out in a footnote to the translation; for bees see *Metaphysics* 980ᵇ22 ff. and *De Partibus Animalium* 648ᵃ5 ff. The remark about imagination conflicts with the implications of 427ᵇ14 ff. as pointed out in the note on that passage.

434^{a}5 ff. makes a distinction between two kinds of imagination, one of which is not possessed by all animals; the implication is that the present remark holds good for only one kind of imagination.)

3. Perceptions are always true, while imaginings are mostly false. (The claim about perception is a gross exaggeration, not uncharacteristic of Aristotle's remarks about perception in these sections; it applies properly only to perception of the special objects. The remark that imaginings are mostly false seems prima facie to go against the suggestion at 427^{b}16 ff. that truth and falsity are irrelevant to imagining. Aristotle presumably has in mind here under 'imaginings' appearances in general. The suggestion that appearances are mostly false connects closely with the next point as does (2).)

4. We speak of things appearing such and such when perception is indistinct. (The text of the last few words of this sentence rendered 'and then it may be either true or false' is uncertain. I do not think that Ross's emendation in the O.C.T., which is noted in a footnote to the translation, is helpful; its relevance is not clear and the subject of the πότερον clause is doubtful. It is possible that the words should be deleted, but I have retained them, despite the fact that a subject, the appearance, has to be supplied. The point is then that appearances when perception is indistinct may be either true or false, i.e. not obviously true. This point then reinforces (2) and (3).)

5. Sights, i.e. probably after-images (cf. 425^{b}24) but perhaps other images also, may occur when our eyes are closed and perception is not functioning.

428^{a}16. It is possible Aristotle means something less strong than conviction by πίστις (*pistis*) e.g. acceptance. For it does not seem obviously true that belief always implies conviction. Aristotle's point also seems to imply in any case that animals cannot have beliefs (on which contrast 434^{a}10 ff.). This too is not obviously so.

The last sentence, which I have included in the text on the ground that it does make an additional point, makes a further claim—that nothing that cannot reason can have beliefs. Aristotle is not of course claiming that beliefs must always be rational, only that nothing can have beliefs unless it is rational. It is possible that this thesis might be defended on some sense of the word 'rational', but whether this would be a sense which Aristotle would accept is another matter. Certainly he thesis requires justification.

428^{a}24. Having argued against the identification of imagination with perception and belief, Aristotle clinches the matter by arguing against the view that it is a combination of the two; he seems here to be trying to refute Plato (*v. Timaeus* 52 a 7, *Sophist* 264 a–b, and cf. *Philebus* 39 b). It is noteworthy that here 'belief' has to take an object (so that it is equivalent to belief in or belief that the object exists or is so) as it commonly does also in Plato. Aristotle argues that on the view that he is criticizing the objects of belief and perception must be the same, and they must not be merely extensionally the same objects. Hence in effect the belief cannot be held on the *basis* of perception.

The main objection follows in the second half of the passage—that in illusions (appearances—here included as usual under imagination) a thing can appear incorrectly despite correct beliefs about it. On the view being criticized this will amount to a person having a true belief that p and a false appearance that $\sim p$ (i.e. the belief plus perception that $\sim p$). Aristotle maintains that when on this view it appears to a person that $\sim p$, he must believe that $\sim p$, and then there are two alternatives, (*a*) that he has given up the belief that p, despite his not having a reason for this, (*b*) he still has it, i.e. this is the belief involved in the appearance. Of these two alternatives:

(*a*) is obviously unsatisfactory, since there is no reason why a man must have given up his true belief about an object when subject to a perceptual illusion about it; and he need not have given it up without reason, for he may still have it. On the other hand:

(*b*) is unsatisfactory, Aristotle claims, because on that view the belief will be true *and* false—true because of the facts and false *ex hypothesi* as the belief involved in the appearance, i.e. p and $\sim p$ will be the same, hence both true and false. The only way in which the belief (which must be what the 'it' refers to throughout) could become false is by a change in the facts, which we might not notice.

It is important to note that on the second alternative (*b*) Aristotle is not saying, as is sometimes supposed, simply that a man cannot hold two contradictory beliefs at the same time. *In general*, the supposition that a man can hold two contradictory beliefs at the same time may be unobjectionable. On the other hand, the first alternative (*a*) does presuppose that a man cannot hold at the same time two contradictory beliefs *about what is before him*. That is why on the view under consideration if he holds the belief that the sun is a foot across, he must have given up the belief that it is bigger than the earth. But why should he? The belief supposedly involved in the appearance is, as noted above, not a belief on the *basis* of a perception. Indeed Aristotle is saying that on the theory being criticized the belief would have no basis. Hence the argument under (*a*). The only alternative is to accept the fact that there is only *one* belief involved in the example, which commits one to (*b*) with the consequence that it must be true in virtue of the facts but false *ex hypothesi*. Thus there is a *reductio ad absurdum* of the theory under examination.

There is a good discussion of the passage by K. Lycos in *Mind* 1964 (N.S. vol. lxiii, no. 292, pp. 496 ff.). Like Lycos, I consider Aristotle's dilemma a valid one. It successfully refutes any theory which attempts to analyse all cases of appearance or seeing-as in terms of beliefs or judgements. On the other hand, I have no doubt that the non-epistemic cases of appearing to which Aristotle draws attention, i.e. cases where something appears *F* without our believing it to be *F*, must be seen and can only be seen against a background of cases where beliefs *are* involved. Our understanding of what it is for something to appear *F* without our believing it to be *F* is dependent on our understanding of what it is for something to appear *F* in such a way that we believe it to be *F*.

428ᵇ10. In the remainder of the chapter Aristotle is concerned with imagination in so far as it is a product of sense-perception and corresponds in characteristics to sense-perception. He reverts to an account of it in something like physical terms, and how truth and falsity attach to it as such is left unclear, despite the assertion that they do. It is not clear how widely 'imagination' is to be construed in these sections, but 428ᵇ25 ff. suggests that it is meant to cover appearances in any sense of the word, i.e. both perceptual appearances and images. Despite Aristotle's earlier remarks at 427ᵇ27 ff. on the close connexion between imagination and thinking, this connexion does not figure at all here.

428ᵇ17. The changes in the text suggested by Bywater provide far better sense than anything that can be extracted from the MS. readings.

Aristotle here lays down the degrees of fallibility to be attached to perception of the three kinds of object distinguished in II. 6. It is noticeable that Aristotle says here that perception of the special objects is 'true or liable to falsity to the least possible extent'. As noted on 418ᵃ11 ff., the example used here is *white*, as opposed to *colour* in the earlier passage. The more specific nature of the example means that Aristotle, whether he realizes it or not, is not really concerned with the same point as he was in the earlier passage. What is contemplated here is the possibility of error over white *vis-à-vis* the other colours, not colour *vis-à-vis* objects of other senses. Aristotle's modification of the thesis of incorrigibility here is no doubt due to a sense of the empirical facts.

The second class of objects referred to are the incidental objects of perception noted earlier, i.e. physical objects. Why does Aristotle put the common objects third in order of increasing liability to error? Do we in fact make more mistakes about, e.g., the size of objects than their colours? It is not, as Ross (edition of *De Anima*, Introd., p. 39) seems to suppose, the point about distance made at 428ᵇ25 ff., since this does not differentiate incidental and common objects. The answer may be the relative nature of size, speed, number, etc., to which Plato appealed at, e.g. *Republic* 479 b, in order to show the unreliability of the world of the senses. They are relative (πρός τι— *pros ti*) in a way in which colour and identity are not. Plato at any rate took this as a reason for attributing fallibility to perception of such qualities, and it may be that Aristotle is doing the same thing here. (Cf. Malebranche's emphasis on the deceptiveness of size, figure, movement, and distance for similar reasons.)

428ᵇ25. Aristotle here removes once again the qualifications which he has put on the infallibility of perception of the special objects, and hence maintains that appearances of these when they are present are true.

428ᵇ30. The etymology used here is dubious (as are many of Aristotle's etymological suggestions).

CHAPTER 4

In this chapter Aristotle turns to the intellect, which is in his view like the senses in many ways. Throughout the chapter he uses with respect to it formulae parallel to those which he uses of the senses, despite the fact that the intellect does not have the same physical conditions and in particular does not have an organ. He also vacillates on the question whether all things or only pure forms or essences are the objects of the intellect. He gives the impression in this chapter of applying the formulae at which he has previously arrived rather mechanically, and he never really resolves the difficulties which result.

429ᵃ13. It is not altogether clear why Aristotle sets up the alternatives in the way in which he does, for, as he makes clear later (at 429ᵃ29; cf. 431ᵃ5), the faculty of sense-perception is not, strictly speaking, affected. The point is that he began his discussion of perception in II. 5 with the notion that perception was a form of being affected, and he then proceeded to put refinements and qualifications on that thesis in a way which leads eventually to a positive rejection of the original idea. The formulae applied to perception in consequence of his original idea are here applied to the intellect, so that it is really the second alternative put forward at the beginning of this section which is in fact accepted. There are, however, difficulties over this which Aristotle never really deals with. These are due to the fact that the formulae invoked here were relevant to sense-perception just because this relies on sense-organs; indeed the reception of form without the matter was seen to be carried out by the sense-organ. The intellect has no organ, and the process therefore remains mysterious in its case. For the same reason the phrase 'that which is capable of perceiving', if it is to refer to something to which the formulae can be applied and also provide a parallel with the intellect, must be essentially ambiguous here (v. below on 429ᵃ29 and on 413ᵇ4 ff.).

429ᵃ18. The intellect must be unmixed with anything, since it thinks everything, and is thus, according to the formula, potentially like all things without being actually such. It must therefore be solely potential, if it is to think all things, and is before thinking nothing actual. If it contained anything actual it could not *become* this, as it must do according to the formula if it is to think it. Aristotle's view of the intellect as pure potentiality is in this way a direct consequence of his view that it must be possible to think of everything. But it leaves the status of the intellect very obscure. How can it exist as a potentiality which is not one of any organ? This is a problem for Aristotle. The best that might be said is that the capacity or potentiality in question is one of the whole man and is dependent on the other faculties which do have organs. (417ᵃ6 says that the faculty of sense-perception also exists only potentially, but it of course depends directly on sense-organs.)

Aristotle adds that those (presumably Platonists) who speak of the soul as the place of forms fit in with his view as long as what they say is reinterpreted in terms of his formula and applied to the intellect.

429ᵃ29. Aristotle must be referring to the faculty of perception in using the '-ikon' terminology here; otherwise the parallel with the intellect cannot be sustained while he is making the distinction between the two.

Cf. 422^{a}20 ff. for destruction of a sense by too intense objects. The way in which the intellect is contrasted with this and what it means to speak of an object as 'especially fit for thought' or 'especially thinkable' is most obscure; presumably thinking of things in the abstract—in respect of their essence or pure form—somehow illuminates the more concrete, so that this becomes more intelligible. The intellect is distinct from the body in the way already suggested, that it is a mere potentiality and has no organ.

The point of the last sentence is to distinguish between the intellect as a mere *dunamis* and the intellect as a *hexis*, between the capacity for thought that a child has and that which a trained thinker has (*v.* on 417^{a}21 and 417^{b}16).

429^{b}10. The reference here is to the familiar Aristotelian distinction between things and their essences (the latter being expressed by the formula 'what it is to be *F*'). In some cases a thing may be identical with its essence, when its individuality and identity are determined by what it is essentially—this not being the case with most things, for which there is much that is accidental or contingent. According to the *Metaphysics* (cf. 1031^{b}11 ff., 1032^{a}4 ff., and especially 1037^{a}33 ff.), the cases in which a thing is identical with its essence consist of the primary instances of substance, i.e. substances in the primary sense of the word. Which things are substances of this kind is a further question. Since, as seen above, their individuality has to be determined by form or essence alone, it comes down in the end to God and the divine intelligences only (for the latter *v.* on 414^{b}16). For these alone are pure form, pure actuality. All other things contain matter, which is responsible for contingency, and at *Metaphysics* 1037^{a}32 Aristotle compares them, as he does here implicitly, to a snub-nose or the snub, which is hollowness in a particular piece of flesh. Snubness is a property of noses which is essential to them in the sense that only noses can be snub (cf. *Posterior Analytics* I. 4 for this kind of essential attribute). In the same way, in things which are composed of matter and form, the particular form is dependent on the particular matter in the way that snubness is dependent on the thing which has it being a nose.

Aristotle suggests that judgements passed on (*a*) essences and (*b*) particulars composed of matter and form must be passed by different faculties or by the same thing 'differently disposed'. The latter alternative tends to suggest that the intellect by which one judges essences, 'what it is to be F', is not after all utterly distinct from the senses. This implies a kind of unity of the faculties, like the unity of the senses implied earlier. That this must be so is in any case implied by the way in which the intellect is dependent for its existence on the senses.

429ᵇ18. Similar considerations apply to mathematical entities, e.g. the straight as a geometrical entity, a straight line. These exist only in abstraction from physical things; they have no independent existence (cf. on 403ᵃ10 and *Metaphysics E.* 1). But they are not pure form or essence; they have matter—an intelligible one (i.e. extension; *v. Metaphysics* 1036ᵃ9 ff.). Hence for the reasons given above they too are like the snub. But the essence of the straight—what it is to be straight (and here Aristotle introduces the general formula for essence; *v.* on 412ᵇ10)—is different; Aristotle suggests duality (i.e. something to do with extension in two directions perhaps; cf. *Metaphysics* 1043ᵃ29 ff. and the Platonic notion of the indefinite dyad).

The last sentence of the passage suggests that the intellect is concerned in different ways according to the extent to which its objects are separable from matter. This sums up the previous discussion.

429ᵇ22. Two problems are raised in this section: (*a*) how can the intellect think if it is unaffected and thinking consists of being affected by something; (*b*) how can the intellect think of itself (this being the problem of self-consciousness raised analogously for the senses in III. 2). The first problem has in effect been dealt with before, but Aristotle goes over the ground again in a way which causes his answer to be slightly mixed up with that to the second problem.

The objections under (*b*) are that if the intellect can think of itself and all its objects are the same in form, all its objects will be like it and have intellect; alternatively, other things will not be so much like it as it like them, so that it will have something actual in it. Both alternatives are unsatisfactory for obvious reasons.

429ᵇ29. In order to deal with the first problem mentioned above Aristotle invokes again the formula given at 429ᵃ13 ff. (cf. 417ᵃ6 for a similar remark about perception, and the notes on this and the following passages, especially 417ᵇ16, for a general discussion of the ideas involved).

The reference to the tablet is meant merely to illustrate the sense of 'potentially' being invoked; there is potentially writing on an empty writing tablet. Aristotle does not mean to draw an analogy between the intellect and a wax tablet.

Aristotle's answer to the problem how the intellect thinks of itself is provided by saying that, as it is without matter and there is an identity between that which thinks and objects of this kind, it is identical with itself as object. The reason for the identity is that actual thought and its object are one and the same—contemplative knowledge being construed, as usual, as an exercise of pure thought. There are, of course, the difficulties already pointed out about what this means, since the formula cannot be interpreted, as was possible in the case of perception, in physical terms (v. also on 417^{b}16). But in any case the restriction to 'things which have no matter' goes against the tenor of the earlier part of the chapter, which tends to take *everything* as a possible object of thought. Here, at any rate, Aristotle seems to identify the intellect with pure thought. It has also to be pointed out that what Aristotle says here does not rule out the possibility that the way in which the intellect does not involve matter may be different from the way in which pure essences as such do not involve matter. (For the general question of the intellect being an object of thought cf. *Metaphysics* 1072^{b}20 and Λ. 9 generally.)

The remark about why the intellect does not always think is parenthetical, suggested presumably by the previous remark about the identity of that which thinks and its object. It is not obvious that Aristotle does consider the question later, except perhaps at the end of Chapter 5.

The final two sentences return to the previous issue, considering now thought of things which do have matter; because they have form, these things have what is potentially an object of thought, and are to this extent themselves thinkable. They will not on that account have intellect in them; for even if the intellect can in a sense be viewed as identical with their form, it is only with the form in separation from the matter and as actual not potential. It receives the form from them (but how?).

In sum, Aristotle wishes to maintain that the intellect in activity is identical with its object (as perception also is); its object is form or essence either in actual separation or as received from physical objects, and Aristotle sometimes restricts his attention to one or other of these alternatives. But what this means in the case of the intellect is extremely obscure, since there is no physical counterpart as in the case of perception. To speak of a sense receiving the form of its object is intelligible in terms of the sense-organ receiving certain qualities of the object, even if this restricts its application. In the case of the intellect, where there is no sense-organ, the whole thing becomes unintelligible, despite the attempts of St. Thomas Aquinas to interpret it in terms of the abstraction of species from phantasms—notions which are in any case foreign to Aristotle. The latter's account of the intellect cannot be said to be happy.

CHAPTER 5

430ᵃ10. This is a much-discussed chapter which introduces the famous or notorious distinction between the active and passive intellects of which St. Thomas Aquinas made so much. The distinction is made by Aristotle only in a metaphysical way; there is no indication in his words that the active intellect plays any role other than that of a metaphysical ground for the actualization of the potentialities which make up the soul. This point is stated at the outset; there must be something in the soul which acts as a cause and brings about the actualization of its potentialities.

The intellect which was discussed in Chapter 4 was said to become all things; it is potentially what its objects are actually and becomes them, *qua* forms, in its actualization. The other intellect which is here postulated by Aristotle (and it must be an intellect if it is to play the role required, because no other faculty of the soul has the necessary generality and universality in its objects) must therefore be entirely actual and thus absolutely distinct from anything material (which could provide potentiality). In this respect its status in the soul is like that of the Prime Mover in the universe at large. Of course even the intellect of Chapter 4 was said to be distinct, unaffected, and unmixed, but it was not 'in essence activity' (cf. also the remarks at 408ᵇ18ff.).

The analogy which Aristotle draws between the active intellect and light is not perhaps immediately perspicuous. As a *hexis* (translated here as 'disposition') light must be something actual; its presence is also a condition for the perception of colours. It makes colours actual by making possible their actualization as objects of perception (*v.* II. 7 generally), and is thus a necessary condition of the perception of colour. In the same way, the activity of the active intellect is a necessary condition of the actualization of the potentialities of the soul, especially the thinking of objects. Although it is a necessary condition of this kind it is not also a sufficient condition and cannot play the role of such. It cannot, e.g., play the role which Aquinas gives to the active intellect in his system—the illumination of the species, the abstraction of them from the phantasms produced by sense and their imposition on the passive intellect. Aquinas derives the notion of the illumination of the species from the analogy with light which Aristotle introduces here, but he misunderstands its import—to illustrate that which makes actualization of potentialities possible.

430ª18. The text of this passage is probably corrupt. The sentence which I have bracketed is repeated at 431ª1. In his edition of the *De Anima* Ross puts brackets round the complete sentence up to 'and at other times not', suggesting deletion. But the last words, which I have left unbracketed, are needed here; they are clearly about the active intellect. It is probable that something else about the active intellect has dropped out before these words, and those from 431ª1 have been substituted for them.

The active intellect must always think because it is actual, not merely potential like the intellect discussed in Chapter 4 (cf. 430ª5 for the remark that *this* does not always think). Hence too, like God, it can have separate existence and is eternal, just because of its lack of potentiality.

The last sentence of the passage has been much discussed and has received many interpretations. One thing seems quite certain—that the 'we' in ª24 cannot be identified with the active intellect. Aristotle is not ascribing to us a disembodied existence in that form. Any transcendent interpretation of this kind must be excluded; there is no ground for it in the text. What then is the object of 'remember'? Is it the functioning of the active intellect? Not very plausibly. The most probable interpretation is that suggested by Hicks—that Aristotle is parenthetically trying to explain why we forget things, although there is an active intellect in us which is always thinking and which there-fore always knows things (cf. too 408ᵇ24 ff.). His answer is that the active intellect is unaffected (and since it would have to be somehow affected if it were responsible for memory, it cannot have this func-tion); but the passive intellect—the intellect responsible for ordinary intellectual functions like memory—can perish, as must the rest of what is ultimately, even if not directly, dependent on the body. On the other hand, the passive intellect is dependent on the active intellect for thinking of any kind, as is stated throughout the chapter.

It must be confessed that this is not the only possible interpretation of the passage. The last five words alone have at least four possible interpretations (*v.* Sir David Ross, *Aristotle*, 4th ed., p. 152). But the interpretation offered here is certainly the least extravagant one and it fits in with everything else that is said in this very brief chapter.

If this interpretation is right, Aristotle provides no grounds here for any kind of belief in personal immortality. The part of the soul which is said to be eternal is a rather abstract entity which has only a metaphysical role to play as a necessary condition of the functioning of the soul. Its status in the soul is somewhat like that of God, on Aristotle's view, in the universe at large; they are both purely actual, and their existence is, in their different ways, a condition of the actualization of the particular potentialities with which they are concerned. It is not therefore surprising that the two have sometimes been erroneously identified. The active intellect, however, may be divine, but it is not itself God.

CHAPTER 6

430ᵃ26. The word ἀδιαίρετος (*adiairetos*) should be translated as 'undivided' rather than 'indivisible' throughout the chapter; it *must* be so translated at 430ᵇ8. The undivided objects in question are the ultimate objects of thought (corresponding to basic concepts, the essences of Chapter 4 in their simplest and basic form as *infimae species*). Their status in relation to thought is said to be like that of the special objects in relation to perception. Hence, to complete the parallel, Aristotle says that they give rise to no falsity. But he is also explicit in saying that truth and falsity are a function of the synthesis of thoughts in judgement (cf. *De Interpretatione* 16ᵃ9 ff., *Metaphysics* 1012ᵃ2 ff., 1027ᵇ17 ff., 1051ᵇ1 ff.). Hence he should, strictly speaking, say here that with respect to thought of undivided objects there is no room for either truth or falsity, and this would by no means amount to a claim for infallibility in this case. (See, however, *Metaphysics* 1051ᵇ 17 ff. which connects attainment of truth with being in contact with something.)

The Empedocles passage which is supposed to supply an analogy for synthesis is DK Fr. 57.

On the addition of the thought of time the *De Interpretatione* ch. 2 says that all verbs signify time in addition—not just verbs in future and past tenses.

In the example involving white and non-white Aristotle is taking the most primitive kind of false statement—the assertion that one thing is its opposite. He maintains that even here there must be, despite the contradiction, a synthesis. He is *not* here asserting that negative statements involve synthesis; the 'not' must be attached to 'white' to make 'non-white' and it is this which white is asserted to be in the example.

Division or separation is the opposite to synthesis. Aristotle maintains that any combination of thoughts into a whole can also be conceived as a separation of thoughts out of a whole. The point is that the kind of thinking in question consists of a complex thought, and the relations between it and its constituents can be described either as synthesis or division, depending on what one takes as the primary component of thought (i.e. the judgement or the concept). This is a question of fundamental importance (cf. Bradley on judgement *v*. idea, Frege and Wittgenstein on statement *v*. name) but Aristotle merely throws out his remark without developing it. Moreover, he does not discuss what kind of synthesis of thoughts judgement consists in; he makes no reference to the notion of predication.

430ᵇ6. This passage has caused the commentators much difficulty and has led to suggestions for emendations. Most of the trouble stems from translating διαιρετός (*diairetos*) and ἀδιαίρετος (*adiairetos*) as 'divisible' and 'indivisible' respectively; for how can one suppose a length to be indivisible? The situation is transformed if one takes the words to mean 'divided' and 'undivided' respectively. Aristotle begins with the distinction between what is actually undivided and what is potentially so (with corresponding cases for the divided). When one thinks of an actually undivided length (which is of course potentially divided, i.e. divisible in principle) one does so in a single undivided thought and in a single unit of time, since the object is one single thing. In that case one cannot divide the thought or its object into halves and ask what one was thinking of in half the time of the whole thought; for there are no actual half-thoughts involved and hence no half-objects or half-times, except potentially in the sense that the whole *could* be divided and so thought of. This latter possibility is then taken up by Aristotle.

In sum, the thought of the whole is said to be one thought, so that we cannot divide it into thoughts of the halves. When there is no actual division the halves do not exist except potentially. Conversely, if one makes a division by thinking of the halves separately there must be two thoughts in two units of time, just as with two quite separate objects or lengths. So, if a whole is compounded out of two halves, the time involved is similarly composite.

430^{b}16. This passage clearly carries on from the preceding and so the transposition of ^{b}14–15 until after ^{b}20 seems quite justified. If one then reads the passage as following on directly after ^{b}6–14 its interpretation ceases to be difficult. (The emendation in ^{b}16 of $\acute{o}$ for $\tilde{\omega}$ is clearly required; the word refers to the length referred to again at ^{b}19.) By 'those things' is meant the half-lengths, etc., of the previous passage, i.e. the divided lengths and times. The object and time of any single thought is not divided except incidentally (i.e. except in a way that has no relevance to the thought—extensionally not intensionally). The wholes and halves are then of course, properly speaking, undivided objects of thought and undivided times. Aristotle then adds that there is something in these undivided objects and times which makes them unities; they have a principle of unity which is provided by the object's being what it is—by its form or essence. In passing, however, he rejects the Platonic view of unity as due to something separate (cf. *Metaphysics* I. 2).

430^{b}14. This, if not a gloss, merely reaffirms the above point with respect to qualitative division.

430^{b}20. Aristotle goes on to bring in another case of something which is undivided, i.e. anything which serves as a limit, e.g. a point or a dividing line. Being limits they are thought and known via what they negate; that is to say that they are thought and known in the way that privations are (cf. 425^{a}19, which says that number is the denial of the continuous).

This leads him to consider our understanding of other privative notions. In conformity with the usual Aristotelian version of the view that knowledge is by opposites, this is said to be due to the fact that the subject is potentially what the object is actually. Although the words 'and the latter must be in it' might stand as a reference to the subject receiving the form of the object, it may be that Aristotle really means to say that the positive quality of which the object previously referred to is a privation must be somehow in the subject, if the privation is to be recognized. If that is so, something must have dropped out of the text.

The last sentence clearly refers to the Aristotelian God, who having no matter is not subject to contraries (cf. *Metaphysics* 1075^{b}20 ff., which says that what is primary has nothing contrary to it because it has no matter).

430ᵇ26. I have accepted the substitution of 'denial' (ἀπόφασις—*apophasis*) for the 'affirmation' (κατάφασις—*kataphasis*) of the MSS. The original reading might be accepted if we could interpret φάσις (*phasis*—here translated as "assertion') as a generic notion like that of 'proposition'.

Aristotle makes explicit here that the undivided objects of thought referred to at the beginning of the chapter are the essences of things (i.e. the 'things without matter'). For the formula 'what it is for it to be what it was' see on 412ᵇ10 ff.

The rest of the passage makes explicit the parallel with sense-perception referred to earlier. For this and comments on it see on 430ᵃ26 ff.

CHAPTER 7

This chapter is a collection of fragments. The text is uncertain in places and the argument often suspect. The same is true of the next chapter.

431ᵃ1. For this passage see also on 430ᵃ18 ff. Aristotle's remarks here on the general priority of the actual to the potential are in conformity with *Metaphysics* Θ. 8.

431ᵃ4. The formula about the relation of the actual to the potential is now reapplied to perception. The potentiality in the individual must be actualized by the object. Here Aristotle finally denies explicitly, despite much of what he has said earlier, that perception, being an activity or actualization, is a form of being affected or of movement generally. For the issues raised here see on 417ᵃ14 ff.

It is not clear whether 'that which can perceive' refers to the faculty or to the sense-organ or animal. 429ᵃ29 speaks of the *faculty* being unaffected (and it must be the faculty to preserve the parallel with the intellect), but here Aristotle seems to be making a somewhat different point.

431ᵃ8. Here the connexion of perception with judgement and hence with assertion is made most explicit. Aristotle also assimilates finding something pleasant to asserting it as good; contrariwise for what is painful. He assumes that pursuit of an object follows directly from the assertion of it as a good (cf. *Nicomachean Ethics* 1139ᵃ21 and what he says about the conclusion of the practical syllogism at *Nicomachean Ethics* 1147ᵃ25 ff.).

For the 'perceptive mean' see on 423ᵇ27 ff. and 424ᵃ28 ff.

The assertion that actual avoidance and desire are the same is a hard saying, even though it is qualified later by the formula asserting difference in *'einai'* (v. on 424ᵃ17 ff.). There is an alternative reading of τοῦτο for ταὐτό—'Avoidance and desire, as actual, are this ...'—but the context suggests that the reading adopted is the right one, especially since the sentence goes on immediately to say that 'that which can desire', 'that which can avoid', and 'that which can perceive' are all identical. (There is, however, not the same difficulty with these, since they can all be construed as referring to the same thing, the animal or the soul.) Aristotle's point over actual avoidance and desire is probably that the same movement can be viewed as a case of seeking one thing and avoiding another (cf. on 425ᵇ26 ff.).

The assertion of the indispensability of images for thought is noteworthy if highly disputable (cf. 432ᵃ9 ff., where there is the only other occurrence of the word αἴσθημα [*aisthēma*—a sense-perception] in the *De Anima*). Aristotle's view about the dependence of thought on images probably arises from his view about the dependence of the higher faculties on the lower ones. But the 'hence' in the last sentence is nevertheless odd, as is indeed the structure of the whole passage.

431ᵃ17. This passage has little to do with the one that precedes it, but it is connected with the one that follows, despite an obvious lacuna in the text. It asserts explicitly that there is ultimately a single faculty of sense (the single mean), although it takes many forms (cf. 426ᵇ8 ff. and the passages of the *Parva Naturalia* mentioned in the notes on this passage and those which follow).

431ᵃ20. This passage returns to the problem of how we discriminate between the objects of different senses, i.e. that discussed at 426ᵇ8 ff., and gives essentially the same answer, since the analogy with the boundary which is invoked here is essentially the same as that with the point invoked at 427ᵃ9 ff.

The passage in general is difficult and has received many interpretations according to the account given of 'these things' at ᵃ22, 'those' at ᵃ23, and '*C*' and '*D*' in ᵃ26–28. (The words suggested for deletion in square brackets are clearly meant to identify *C* and *D* with 'those'; this is correct even if the comment is a gloss.) It seems fairly clear that 'these things' must be the sweet and the hot. These are one (a) by analogy, i.e. in their relations to the corresponding unified senses, and (b) in number, i.e. in that the thing perceived is both sweet and hot. It might be inferred from the sentence beginning 'for what difference does it make . . .' that 'those' are the white and the black; alternatively it might be that they are the opposites of sweet and hot and that Aristotle goes on to work out the relations between all these. But I think that in fact 'those' refers back to something that has dropped out in the lacuna at the end of the previous paragraph, i.e. the senses concerned. (For other interpretations see Hicks, pp. 531 ff. and Ross, pp. 305 ff. The interpretation which I have adopted is essentially that of Neuhaeuser mentioned by Hicks. The objections that Hicks raises against it arise from his general confusion of the unified faculty of sense with the common sense.)

On this interpretation, Aristotle goes on to say that it makes no difference whether the objects are merely different or are opposites; there will still have to be a unity. As the objects A and B are to each other so the senses or the perceptions C and D are to each other. (By 'alternando' Aristotle means 'as A is to C, so B is to D', and this clearly also holds.) Now A and B can belong to one thing, so that they can be said to be numerically one but different in 'einai' (v. again on 424^a 17 ff.). The same will be true of the perceptions C and D, so that there will be numerically one faculty of perception with different manifestations. The same also applies to other senses and perceptions, and it makes no difference whether A and B are opposites or merely different (cf. 426^{b}29 ff. and De Sensu 449^{a}3 ff.).

(In the O.C.T. Ross emends 'CD . . . AB' to 'CA . . . DB' on the grounds that if C and D are opposites they could not both belong to the same thing [and similarly for A and B]. But on the view which I have put forward the point that Aristotle seems to be making is that they *could* so belong. In any case, on Ross's view, according to which C and D are, e.g., the sweet and the bitter [so that CA is the sweet and the white] the alternative proposed in the last sentence would make CA be the sweet and the bitter, which would, on his view, still be objectionable.)

431^{b}2. Aristotle now returns to the issues left off at 431^{a}17. The intervening two paragraphs may indeed be an interpolation of some kind. Aristotle never explains further the way in which images function like sense-perceptions in connexion with avoidance and pursuit. It is

perhaps noteworthy that here 'that which can think' must refer to
the animal or man, since it is he who is moved, not the faculty. The
'those' of ᵇ3 are the forms of actual objects (ᵇ2) which the animal
or man perceives.

The example of the beacon is not meant to illustrate the function
of images but to provide a case to illustrate the role of perception in
initiating actions (but what on earth is the action in question?); this
is to be compared with the role of images which is referred to next.
'There' and 'here' in ᵇ9 must mean in the case of perception and in the
case of thought respectively. (If the words $\tau\hat{\eta}$ $\kappa o\iota\nu\hat{\eta}$ ['by the common
sense'] are to be retained at ᵇ5, they will somehow have to have close
connexion with 'seeing it moving', since the common sense could not
be that by which one recognizes the hostility of the beacon. On the
other hand, it would be odd to speak of *seeing* the motion by the
common sense [at any rate without qualification]. It is therefore best
to treat the expression as a gloss and to delete it.)

To say that truth and falsity are in the same genus as the good and
the bad is but to say that they are parallel; they fall together in a
table of opposites. In saying that truth and falsity are not relative to
anyone, Aristotle is quite correct. Good and bad, at least in the sense
in question here, are (if they are to affect action) good and bad for the
person concerned, and thus relative.

431ᵇ12. This passage and the one that follows it are not connected with
what precedes them or indeed with anything else in the chapter.
They have more connexion with Chapter 6.

For the snub see on 429ᵇ10. As far as concerns mathematical
entities which exist only in abstraction (cf. 429ᵇ18 and 403ª10),
Aristotle is simply saying here that while they are not really separately
existing entities one thinks of them as such.

(For 'spoken of as in abstraction' cf. 432ª5; it is not that mathematical entities are spoken of in abstraction, but that they exist in
abstraction and are so spoken of. See on 412ª22 for the type of expression.)

431ᵇ17. The promise made in the last sentence is, as far as can be
seen, not carried out. It is not altogether clear why the problem arises
in the form in which Aristotle expresses it here. The main problem is
rather one concerning the relation between the intellect which can
think immaterial entities and the body—a problem which was not
satisfactorily dealt with in Chapter 4.

CHAPTER 8

This brief chapter has acquired a certain reputation as summing up Aristotle's views. On closer examination, however, it appears, like the previous chapter, rather scrappy and perhaps crude. Certainly it is too early in the book to sum up, since the treatment of movement is still to come. It is reasonable to have doubts about its authenticity, at any rate as a chapter in this book.

431^{b}20. This merely sums up what has been said many times before about perception, thought, and their objects.

431^{b}24. This passage provides more details about the relation between perception, thought, and their objects. But the division mentioned in the first sentence seems unnecessarily geometrical. Why must the potential correspond to the potential, and the actual to the actual, in this way, and what is the significance of the correspondence? However, what Aristotle goes on to say in the next sentence is certainly in conformity with his general doctrine.

The hand is a tool of tools in the sense that it is used in order to use tools; but the parallel between this and a form of forms provides more elegance than illumination. The point is presumably that the intellect and sense are forms for the reason that the soul in general was said to be at the beginning of Book II, i.e. because it is the capacity of a living thing for exercising its functions. But what is the sense of 'form of forms'? The point is probably that since the intellect and senses receive forms, they are potentially those forms and are thus a potentiality for becoming forms. For this reason they are described in this very abstract way as a form of forms and a form of objects of perception respectively.

In ^{b}26 the use of the words 'in the soul' with 'that which can perceive' and 'that which can know' indicates that here at least the phrases refer to the faculty in question, and it is this which is said to be potentially its objects. Thus this passage is the exception to the rule given in the notes on 418^{a}3, where it was said that the formula applies to the organ of the faculty. The snag, as has appeared since in many places, is that the rule cannot apply to the intellect in any case, however much it may apply to perception.

432^{a}3. This paragraph encapsulates what is sometimes referred to as Aristotle's empiricism, and is the source of the dictum that there is

nothing in the intellect that was not previously in the senses. The
initial statement may seem to contradict other statements elsewhere
concerning, e.g., God's separate existence, not to speak of that of other
entities. In fact the passage has the same indefiniteness on this matter
as the attitude towards theology expressed in parts of *Metaphysics E.* 1.

For the role of images see on 431ª8 ff. and 431ᵇ2 ff. Aristotle means
by 'imagination' here simply the having of images.

The passage tails off into a query about the relation between the
simplest thought and images, a query prompted perhaps by the fact
that he has distinguished between imagination and discursive thought
by saying that the latter involves a combination of thoughts. His
answer is, rightly enough, that thought is always thought, even if
dependent on images.

CHAPTER 9

This chapter returns to the more systematic account of the faculties
of the soul which was abandoned after Chapter 6 according to our
present text and replaced by a series of fragmentary and often unre-
lated discussions which have something of the mark of an interpolation. The opening section of this chapter merely sets the stage for a
discussion of the problem of locomotion.

432ª22. Aristotle rightly objects to the kind of tripartite theory of
the soul put forward by Plato in the *Republic* 434 d ff. and also to the
division into rational and irrational parts, which the *Magna Moralia*
1182ª23 attributes to Plato but which is said at *Nicomachean Ethics*
1102ª26 ff. to be a popular distinction.

The status of the imagination has always been a problem for
Aristotle (cf. the discussion of III. 3). Here Aristotle agrees that it is
different from other faculties in '*einai*', but is uncertain whether or not
it is coincident or numerically the same as any of them (this implies
the familiar distinction discussed under 424ª17 ff.). His difficulties
on this and similar points might rightly provoke doubts on the whole
faculty approach to the soul.

For the distinction between kinds of desire see on 413ᵇ16 and
414ª32. Similar distinctions are made at *Nicomachean Ethics* 1111ᵇ10 ff.,
Rhetoric 1369ª1 ff., *Politics* 1334ᵇ22.

For breathing in and out see the *De Respiratione* and for sleep and
waking the *De Somno*.

432ᵇ13 ff. Aristotle differentiates between that which is responsible for movement and the faculties of nutrition, perception, and intellect in characteristic ways—by appealing to counter-examples to the thesis that they might be identified with each other.

The thesis that nature does nothing without reason is a common expression of the teleological principle in Aristotle.

432ᵇ26. The suggestion that all animal movement is a function of avoidance and pursuit is notable, although it is scarcely acceptable; Aristotle's account of the motivation of behaviour is on the whole fairly simple-minded. It is also worth noting the suggestion that mere contemplation of something frightening or pleasant may have a physical effect, without calling out actual fear or pleasure. The physical effect is presumably a form of excitement (cf. an analogous statement about imagination at 427ᵇ16 ff.).

433ª1. The intellect mentioned here is presumably practical but is by itself insufficient to produce movement. There must be wants which in the incontinent man take possession of him. But wants too are not sufficient by themselves, for continent people let reason guide them.

CHAPTER 10

433ª9. To allow his account to cover animals, Aristotle has to extend his usual notion of the intellect to cover the imagination, if it is to be a candidate for being the cause of movement in animals. Any intellect of this kind must be in any case practical in the sense that it must consider matters in relation to an end. Hence the object of the desire, the end, is what we start from in calculating means to it, and we work back until we come to something which is immediately relevant and is therefore the starting-point for action (cf. *Nicomachean Ethics* 1112ᵇ11 ff.).

433ª17. Having been through these considerations, Aristotle now gives prime importance to desire in the initiation of movement, presumably on the dubious grounds that there has in the end to be just one cause. Intellect cannot function practically without desire, while the latter can so function without reasoning, as in irrational wants. It might be objected that this does not make desire sufficient and necessary as the cause of movement since Aristotle has not eliminated all forms of the intellect as part causes of movement (cf.

the role given to the imagination earlier). Presumably even the incontinent must have some *idea* of what they want.

It is to be noted that here as at 432ᵇ3 ff. desire (ὄρεξις—*orexis*) is the generic notion; wishing (βούλησις—*boulēsis*) covers rational desires; and wanting (ἐπιθυμία—*epithumia*) irrational ones.

433ª26. That intellect is always right is a characteristic exaggeration. Presumably Aristotle says this in order to differentiate the concept of *the* good as an end from the concept of apparent good which might be put down to the imagination. The good which is not practicable probably includes things like God which might be called good in some sense but are not possible ends of human action. The practicable is something which is not necessarily so and hence cannot be an object of science. This point is made frequently in the *Nicomachean Ethics*; ethics is concerned with things that can be otherwise.

433ª31. The reference here to wanting and passion suggests that this is another side attack on Plato with exactly the same point as at 432ª22 ff.

433ᵇ5. Having claimed that desire is *the* cause of movement in animals, Aristotle has to deal with the point that desires may conflict (rational *v.* irrational—reason *v.* wants). He does this by means of the suggestion that while there may be many desires responsible for any given movement they will be all one in kind, and so the movement will be a product of the faculty of desire as such. Hence they will have in a sense one cause. Aristotle's preoccupation with the problem of which *faculty* is paramount in movement, rather than with that of what exactly is the cause of any given movement exemplifies his tendency to think of the faculties as kinds of agency. He certainly speaks on occasion of faculties *doing* things.

433ᵇ13 ff. Aristotle now sums up the constituents in the production of movement. (1) The practical good (something unmoved) produces movement in (2) the faculty of desire, which itself moves (3) the animal by (4) a means which is bodily. The last is discussed briefly in the next section in terms of the mechanics of bodily movement through the ball-and-socket joint (cf. *De Motu Animalium* 698ª14 ff., 701ᵇ1 ff.). The two parts of the joint meet at a point, so that they can be said to be spatially inseparable, although the functions of the two parts are different and so in consequence are their definitions (*v.* again on 424ª17 ff. for the formula).

The analogy of the circle is to be explained by the consideration that a circle is supposed to be produced by a movement round a fixed point, the centre. So in bodily movement one point must be fixed, and in relation to it the rest moves.

The two kinds of imagination distinguished at the end are respectively that which is a kind of thinking and that which is responsible for perceptual illusions, etc. (cf. III. 3 and 434ª5 ff.).

Aristotle's account of animal and human movement is vitiated by a failure to make a proper distinction between action or behaviour and the bodily movement which a physiologist might be concerned with. In consequence, for a great deal of the time he appears to be looking for the *causes* of movement, without making clear whether this is action or mere bodily movement. At other times he seems to be looking for the factors which will be necessary in any proper account of behaviour, and to be asking what psychological faculties are presupposed. But he also runs the two kinds of account together on occasion, so that the faculties in question appear to function as agencies of some kind. It is in general, however, the causal account that is uppermost in Aristotle's mind, and there is no doubt that his thinking on the matter is relatively crude. This is particularly so when it comes to establishing the connexion between the psychological factors and the bodily mechanism. He thinks it sufficient to say at the end of the section beginning 433ᵇ13 that it must be investigated 'among the functions common to body and soul'; he is regrettably vague about the whole matter.

CHAPTER 11

433ᵇ31. Imperfect animals (here equivalent to the lowest forms of animals) are not here denied imagination. Aristotle's argument entails that they have it but only in an indeterminate form.

434ª5. The last words of this section are obscure but involve the notion that one must be able to synthesize issues to have the idea of a single standard in terms of which the action that one is to take must be assessed.

434ª10. That animals have beliefs is asserted here despite what is implied by 428ª19 ff. The point that Aristotle is making is that they have beliefs about the end to be pursued although they cannot deliberate.

In the following I have retained the MSS. text, although the general sense of Bywater's emendation adopted by the O.C.T. need not be vastly different. On the MSS. reading 'desire' is initially opposed to wish (as irrational to rational desire) and then is used to cover it. The point is that in incontinence a man may be driven, first in one direction and then in another, by different kinds of desires. The three motions referred to are probably those of the two desires, one of which is predominant and so effective over the other, and the product of the two.

In the above I have adopted the simple hypothesis that the comparison with the ball is based either on the idea that a ball bounces to and fro like the desires or on the idea that it is similarly thrown to and fro in a game. But there is an alternative view, due originally to Themistius, which interprets σφαῖρα (*sphaira*) as 'sphere' (i.e. heavenly sphere), and introduces complicated notions of celestial mechanics (for which see Hicks, pp. 569 ff.). I do not think this would be so appropriate a simile.

Aristotle finally points out that knowledge as such is not affected in the above process, merely the desires (cf. the Socratic position on incontinence). He develops this point in the next section along the lines of the so-called practical syllogism. It is the acceptance of the minor premiss, which is particular in one way or another, which is influenced by desire. (Cf. *Nicomachean Ethics* 1146ᵇ35 ff., *De Motu Animalium* 701ª13 ff., and especially *Nicomachean Ethics* 1147ᵇ9 ff. for the effect on and of the minor premiss.) It is clear in fact that on this construction both premisses are responsible for movement.

CHAPTER 12

In the last two chapters Aristotle sums up the functions of the soul as functions of life, with special reference to animal life, for which perception is a necessary condition. The teleological emphasis is notable, as is the reference to the physiological conditions for the exercise of the functions in question.

434ª27 ff. Aristotle argues here for the biological necessity of perception for an animal. The argument is rather tortuous. It begins by considering the necessity of perception for the movement of non-stationary animals, in order that they may get nourishment, but it goes off in the middle to argue that nothing can have intellect and not have perception. The argument on the latter point is that it would not be to the advantage of either soul or body to have the one and not the other. (Why it *need* be to their advantage is not made clear, but it is part of the general presuppositions of the passage.)

The significance of the question posed at ᵇ5—'Why would it have it?'—if it is read without a 'not', is 'Why would a non-stationary but generated animal have intellect but not perception?' Aristotle's answer is that it would have to be for some purpose; but, he goes on, it could not be so, since thinking depends on perception. The MSS. are divided on whether one should read a 'not' in the question. With the 'not' something like the same sense could be extracted from it, but more awkwardly—'Why would such an animal not have perception and yet have intellect?'

434ᵇ9. The argument for the necessity of touch is in part somewhat obscure. Aristotle is probably playing on a certain ambiguity in the word 'touch'. The point is that if the animal body is touched by other bodies, it must be able to touch other bodies, i.e. be capable of perceiving them by touch, if it is to survive. It must, as he goes on to say, be capable by this means of taking some things and avoiding others.

434ᵇ18. The paramount importance of touch and taste for an animal is here emphasized strongly, but it is also to be noted that the other senses are said to be necessary for the well-being of the animal.

434ᵇ29. This section is meant to provide an explanation of how perception through a medium takes place—the issue raised at the end of the previous section. It is assumed once more that perception is a form of being affected and therefore of change. The examples at the end are presumably meant to illustrate the point that things can be altered while remaining in the same place; but they are not very helpful in illustrating the form of change involved in perception.

435ᵃ5. The view rejected here, which in fact makes reference to a general theory of perception, involving the idea that something issues from the eye in vision as well as from the object, is to be found in Empedocles, Fr. 84, Plato, *Timaeus* 45 b ff. (cf. *De Sensu* 437ᵇ10 ff.).

CHAPTER 13

435ᵃ11 ff. Cf. 422ᵇ34 ff. The argument here is that the senses, apart from touch, might rely on the elements other than earth. But they are not independent of touch. And, he goes on to say in the next section, touch cannot rely only on earth. It is too complicated for this. Hence the animal body, which must have touch, cannot be composed of a single element (though it is not clear why it might be thought to be so composed). The argument depends on the ideas of the necessity of touch for animal life and its complexity as a sense.

435ᵇ4. For the destruction of a sense-organ by excess in an object see on 422ᵃ20 and for the necessity of touch for an animal see on 413ᵇ4. In earlier references to the first point the destruction of a sense-organ amounted to the destruction, if only temporary, of the functioning of the sense-organ. Also the earlier references to the necessity of touch for an animal in II. 2 and 3 were to the effect that anything that lacked touch would not *be* an animal. Here Aristotle seems to argue differently. He seems here to say that excess in objects of touch literally destroys the sense-organ and hence the animal. But temporary loss of the power to perceive by touch would not necessarily lead to death, nor would some more serious cases of damage. The argument could be formally valid only if Aristotle is arguing that the life of an animal is causally dependent on touch, and the truth of the conclusion would then depend on whether it was as a matter of fact true that destruction of the sense-organ of touch leads to death. It has to be remembered here that, in so far as Aristotle has said what the sense-organ of touch is, the suggestion is that it is something internal—the heart. If Aristotle is arguing, as seems to be the case, in causal terms, this would be in line with the general tenor of the argument in these last two chapters. It fits very much less well with the treatment of the status of touch in animals in II. 2 and 3; although it makes superficially a similar point to the one made there, the issues are in fact quite different. Whether Aristotle thinks that he is making the same point is not so clear.

From what has been said about individual points in the last two chapters it is a plausible inference that their origin is different from those which immediately precede them and perhaps from the bulk of the *De Anima*. Their approach is different; they go back to the idea that perception is a form of being affected, and the treatment of the way in which touch is essential to animal life does not fit in with other things said on this matter. On the other hand, the discussion in these chapters is not radically inconsistent with what is to be met with elsewhere in the *De Anima*. Indeed, some aspects of the emphasis on biological utility to be found here merely give greater stress to what has been there all along. Nevertheless, there is sufficient difference between the chapters and what precedes to provoke the question whether they were not added at some stage to what is the main fabric of the *De Anima*.

SOME RECENT APPROACHES
TO ARISTOTLE'S *DE ANIMA*

CHRISTOPHER SHIELDS

I

The first edition of Hamlyn's translation and commentary immediately preceded a sustained, intensive investigation into the philosophical issues raised by the terse, pregnant text of the *De Anima*. As the ever-expanding literature on the *De Anima* enters its third decade since Hamlyn, it may prove useful to take stock by surveying some of the dominant themes of inquiry as a first step toward philosophical reappraisal.

Scholarly opinion concerning even the most basic tenets of the *De Anima* is alarmingly diverse. It is agreed by all that Aristotle regards the soul as the form of the body (*DA* 414^{a}14–19). But agreement ends here: it is unclear whether this commitment to hylomorphism implicitly promotes a form of materialism or of dualism, or is perhaps somehow *sui generis*. There is correspondingly little agreement on the tenability of Aristotle's hylomorphism. Several scholars, including Ackrill (1972–3/1979) and Burnyeat (1992), have forcefully challenged the credibility of Aristotle's view, arguing that the deployment of Aristotle's form/matter distinction in the philosophy of mind is at best infelicitous. These challenges have been met with rejoinders, and the ensuing discussion has led to some new ground-level reassessments of the precise philosophical commitments contained in Aristotle's psychological writings.

In this review essay I shall focus on Aristotle's hylomorphism, and especially on the ontological commitments of this view. I begin by recapitulating the main avenues of approach to his hylomorphism, and by offering limited assessments of each. I also consider the principal challenges to this view, and locate the most promising lines of defence (§ II). In concentrating on hylomorphism, I set aside independent discussion of a host of issues from the *De Anima*, including its prefatory historical remarks, its account of desire, and its philoso-

157

phy of action. Still, no investigation into hylomorphism can proceed altogether detached from Aristotle's accounts of the special faculties of the soul: indeed, the *De Anima* is much more concerned to analyse the individual capacities of the soul than to articulate and defend hylomorphism in the abstract. Consequently, I also review a small but representative portion of the literature on perception (*aisthēsis*), imagination (*phantasia*), and mind (*nous*) (§ III).

II

Aristotle rejects a central tenet of Plato's philosophy of mind by holding unequivocally that the soul cannot be separated from the body (*DA* 413^{a}3–5). His commitment to the non-separability of the soul seems reasonable in light of his claiming first that the soul and body are related as form and matter (*DA* 414^{a}14–19), and second that the form and its proximate matter are somehow one (*Meta.* 1045^{b}16–21). Given these claims, we might expect him to embrace some form of materialism, since forms, and so souls, can be the same as bodies only if they are themselves material. He frustrates this easy expectation, however, since he is reluctant to endorse any simple, straightforward form of materialism. First, in the same chapter of the *De Anima* in which he eschews inquiry into whether the soul and body are one (*DA* 412^{b}6–9), he insists that the soul is not the body, on the grounds that the body, unlike the soul, is a substrate (*hupokeimenon*) (*DA* 412^{a}15–19). Second, he maintains that the distinctive capacity of the human soul, mind (*nous*), is immaterial (*DA* 429^{a}24–5), and may hold a similar thesis regarding perception (*aisthēsis*). Finally, despite his rejection of Platonism, Aristotle nevertheless dangles the possibility of *post mortem* existence by making *nous* not only immaterial but separable, explicitly affirming that the active mind (*nous poiētikos*) is deathless and sempiternal (*DA* 430^{a}23).

Precisely because Aristotle variously emphasizes the soul's connection to the body and its distinct, formal character, scholars have disputed the interpretation of his hylomorphism, promulgating non-equivalent and often incompatible views. It may of course turn out that the relevant texts provide no resolution to such scholarly disagreements, perhaps because they simply underdetermine the issue, or indeed because they are themselves internally inconsistent. Or it may be, as some have urged, that all attempts to translate Aristotle's idiom into our own will necessarily be frustrated, because of a conceptual mismatch between his framework of inquiry and that of all post-Cartesian philosophies of mind. This need not entail that Aristotle's programme has no worth; on the contrary, if true, his assumptions and conclusions might equally lead to a reappraisal of the issues that have come to define contemporary philosophy of mind.

Such global consequences would be arresting. It seems clear, then, that before we offer such strident claims, we should appreciate the main sources of difficulty for our understanding Aristotle's hylomorphism. These clearly flow in part from the intractability of Aristotle's texts. Even so, a careful look at the scholarship on the *De Anima* reveals another hindrance to consensus: there is no settled or received understanding of what is meant by characterizing Aristotle as a materialist or as a dualist, and consequently no clear appreciation of what is meant by suggesting that his view is *sui generis*, that it cannot be assimilated to any variety of materialism or dualism.

For clarity's sake, we can characterize a Platonic dualist as one who holds that souls are immaterial entities capable of existing independently of the body (although Plato's views evolve, this is clearly the view accepted *inter alia* in the *Phaedo*). A materialist, by contrast, holds that psychological states are also material states (so that, for example, the belief that Vienna is pretty is also some neural state n). This is a generic characterization, and because many commentators have sought to formulate Aristotle's views more precisely as some particular variety of materialism, it will also be useful to distinguish strong from weak materialism about the mental: (i) strong materialism holds that mental-state types are identical with physical-state types; while (ii) weak materialism holds that every human mental-state token is also a physical-state token. It is clear that (i) entails (ii), but not *vice versa*; weak, but not strong, materialism is compatible with the logical possibility of a mental state's being realized by some non-physical system. Neither set of options is exhaustive.

As formulated, Platonic dualism and generic materialism are mutually exclusive but not exhaustive: one could be a dualist without being a Platonic dualist, and one could be a materialist without embracing some specifications of the generic formulation of materialism provided. To understand this, one need only reflect that strong and weak materialism do not exhaust varieties of materialism: as we shall see, some of the best formulations of Aristotle's hylomorphism may be taken as attempts to locate his view somewhere on the continuum defined by the termini these positions provide. In any case, it seems accepted by all, or nearly all, that Aristotle is neither a Platonic dualist nor a strong materialist. Perhaps most distinctive of recent scholarship on hylomorphism is its tendency to converge around the threshold between the weakest forms of materialism and the weakest forms of dualism.

In surveying the positions offered for Aristotle together with the passages variously cited in their support, it becomes evident that reasonable cases can be made for distinct and even incompatible interpretations. It is therefore not unreasonable to wonder whether Aristotle decisively endorses materialism or dualism, or, if he does, to wonder whether he decisively endorses any finely tuned variety of either; nor is it unreasonable to wonder in general whether his position can be assimilated to any recognizably modern position. It is possible that he has failed to pose for himself the questions he would need to answer in order for us to make these sorts of determinations. For this reason, it is worth considering at the outset the prominent suggestion that Aristotle's philosophy of mind is somehow *sui generis*.

(1) *Hylomorphism as* sui generis. Sorabji has advanced the view that Aristotle's position is *sui generis* and so 'not to be identified with the positions of more recent philosophers' (1974/1979, p. 43).[1] This is an interesting and important suggestion, since if true it will recommend serious meta-theoretical reflection about the array of positions on mind–body relations taken by contemporary philosophers. Sorabji seeks to establish the uniqueness of Aristotle's approach by contrasting it with Cartesian dualism and several varieties of contemporary materialism. His account of Aristotle is therefore an arresting one, insofar as it holds out the possibility that Aristotle shows how post-Cartesian taxonomies in the philosophy of mind are misguided, perhaps because they tacitly incorporate false presuppositions about our mental terrain, or formulate the important questions about mind and body by relying on a noxious conceptual apparatus.[2]

But it is questionable whether Sorabji's method of contrasts is sufficient for his purposes. First, Sorabji's claim is more or less ambitious depending on the sense in which he regards Aristotle's position as *sui generis*. He initially portrays Aristotle's view as *sui generis* in a robust sense, such that it highlights the conceptual indefensibility of any clear distinction between materialism and immaterialism

(p. 43). Yet after contrasting Aristotle's view with contemporary materialism, Sorabji seems to settle for a comparatively anaemic thesis by representing hylomorphism as an otherwise unespoused form of materialism: 'Aristotle improves on some present-day materialists' by refusing to identify the soul with the body (p. 55). Even this milder thesis, if true, will hold considerable interest for us. If Aristotle's hylomorphism is *sui generis* in this sense, then we stand to learn something from him by coming to recognize a form of materialism which we had otherwise overlooked.

There are grounds for scepticism about the milder thesis as well. If he is a materialist who refuses to identify souls with bodies, then Aristotle joins forces with the many contemporary materialists who hold that mental states are constituted by physical states without being identical with them. Sorabji's interpretation consequently gives us no reason to regard Aristotle's hylomorphism as a *sui generis* form of materialism. *A fortiori* it gives us no reason to regard Aristotle's views as *sui generis* in any more robust sense. Hence, it remains an open question whether one can appropriately regard Aristotle's views as occupying some identifiable place in a familiar taxonomy of views in the contemporary philosophy of mind.

(2) *Hylomorphism as materialism.* If Sorabji is wrong to characterize Aristotle's views as in any sense *sui generis*, he is not thereby wrong to regard him as a particular sort of materialist. Indeed, the real import of Sorabji's position is to regard Aristotle as a sophisticated materialist, who makes philosophically fruitful use of the notion of constitution in describing mind–body relations.[9] The thought that bodies constitute souls in the way that a quantity of clay constitutes a vase is a first approximation of a weak form of materialism. Consequently, Sorabji's view agrees with what is clearly the dominant trend of interpretation, that hylomorphism is a form of weak materialism.

What feature of hylomorphism requires materialism? Most commentators presume that Aristotle's hylomorphism must amount to some form of materialism since it is precisely calculated to avoid Platonic dualism and explicitly affirms the non-separability of soul and body (*DA* 413^{a}3–^{b}6). A clear example of this sort of reasoning is provided by Barnes (1971–2/1979), who infers what he calls a weak form of physicalism directly from the thesis that the soul is not separable from the body; indeed, he maintains (p. 35) that Aristotle's commitment to non-separability 'states' a form of weak physicalism, which he characterizes as:

$$\psi a \rightarrow \phi a$$

where ψ is some mental predicate and ϕ is some physical predicate.[4] Thus, if a is the belief that Vienna is a handsome city, then a is also some physical state, most likely in human beings some neural state. Barnes's view is a form of materialism because it commits Aristotle to the position that all psychic states are also material states; it is *weak* materialism because it does not entail that every mental-state type (being-ψ) is identical with some physical-state (being-ϕ), and thus allows that mental states can be realized by a variety of distinct physical states.

However weak, Barnes's version of physicalism is not entailed by Aristotle's commitment to non-separability. While it is certainly true that in denying the soul's separability Aristotle rejects Platonic dualism, according to which the soul is both an immaterial substance and separable from the body, this denial does not by itself entail any form of materialism. For it is compatible with the view that mental states require physical states as supervenience bases, even though they are not themselves physical states.[5] That is, Aristotle's commitment to non-separability is compatible with a view according to which mental states are ontologically dependent on states of the body, even though they are not constituted by them. Hence, an unaugmented commitment to non-separability underdetermines the issue.

Of course, materialist interpretations of Aristotle's hylomorphism find many other sources of textual support. Beyond insisting on the non-separability of soul and body, Aristotle claims in addition that the soul and body are one, and one in the strictest sense. As he says,

> It is therefore not necessary to inquire whether the soul and the body are one, just as it is [not necessary to inquire] whether the wax and its shape [are one], nor generally whether the matter of each thing, and that of which it is the matter [are one]. For while one and being are spoken of in many ways, actuality is most strictly [spoken of in this way]. (*DA* 412^{b}6–9; my translation)

Since the soul is the actuality of the body (*DA* 412^{a}21), one would expect the soul and body to be one in the strictest sense; thus, at least initially, Aristotle invites us to regard soul and body as identical. Still, it is worth reflecting on Aristotle's illustration of the sort of unity he has in mind. He offers the wax of a candle and its shape as analogous to the matter of a body and its soul. The analogy may seem ill-suited on several counts: most notably, the shape of a candle is evidently a universal,[6] while its wax is a spatio-temporal particular, and so not logically repeatable. If this is correct, the shape and the wax can hardly be one thing, and therefore can hardly be identical. Consequently, Aristotle's analogy initially undermines rather than supports the contention that soul and body are to be identified, even if it provides an illustration of the soul's non-separability from the body.

The canonical texts invoked in attributing materialism to Aristotle thus fall short of committing him to that view. They suggest an outlook comfortable with a materialist orientation, while not actually entailing any such settled position. These particular texts, however, do not exhaust the available evidence in support of a materialist rendering of hylomorphism. Charles (1984) finds other evidence committing Aristotle to 'ontological materialism', a view he characterizes thus: 'For any true psychological description of the world (*either* a description of the psychological phenomena *or* a description making use of psychological vocabulary) there is some state of affairs characterisable employing only physical vocabulary such that: the obtaining of the physical state is sufficient (but not causally sufficient) for the truth of the psychological description' (p. 214). Charles's interpretation represents a refinement of Barnes's insofar as it admits the possibility that a physical state could be (non-causally) sufficient for a mental state without actually constituting it. But it is for this very reason still weaker than Barnes's form of weak physicalism, and is in fact compatible with views carrying no commitment to materialism as such.[7]

Nevertheless, Charles offers a sophisticated argument calculated to establish that Aristotle is in fact a materialist. On his interpretation of Aristotle's theory of action, every intentional action is caused by some necessitating bodily movement (1984, pp. 215–16), which is itself necessitated by some set of physical processes. At the same time, an agent's desires efficiently cause the bodily movements requisite for action (citing *EN* 1111^{a}22–3 and *DA* 433^{b}21–2, 433^{a}31 ff.). Thus, according to Aristotle, both psychological and physiological conditions are efficient causes of action, while efficient causes are sufficient conditions. This presents Aristotle with a choice: either bodily movements are in a systematic way causally overdetermined or the psychological causes of behaviour are also physiological events. Charles adduces evidence to show that Aristotle opts for the second alternative. He suggests that for Aristotle physical effects must have physical causes (PC), a principle which entails that a psychological state 'cannot be a cause of bodily movement unless it is enmattered in some physical state which necessitates the bodily movement as its essential cause' (1984, p. 219). Hence, his argument relies crucially on locating a commitment to (PC), which he finds in *De Motu Animalium* 703ᵃ18–29. Charles evidently relies on 703ᵃ24–5, where Aristotle says 'whatever is going to impart motion without itself undergoing alteration must be of this type [viz. of the so-called connate pneuma, or *sumphuton pneuma*[8]]' (*dei de to mellon kinein mē alloiōsei toiouton einai*). But this passage neither contains nor entails (PC): it claims only that whatever can impart motion without undergoing qualitative change must have the sort of plasticity that the connate pneuma has, thereby leaving open the possibility that something could be of the same type as the connate pneuma, and so have the requisite characteristics, without being a physical cause.[9] Thus, this passage does not commit Aristotle to (PC), and therefore does not provide the premiss Charles needs to show that hylomorphism can be understood only as a form of ontological materialism.[10]

In light of the anti-Platonic sentiment abundant in Aristotle's philosophy of mind, Charles is surely justified in seeking to reduce hylomorphism to a form of materialism. Still, Aristotle's causal commitments do not actually resolve the issue decisively in this direction. Consequently, despite considerable textual evidence suggesting such a conclusion, Aristotle's hylomorphism does not obviously collapse into some type of materialist theory, however weak. To be sure, commentators have, not unreasonably, sought to understand Aristotle's hylomorphism as a form of weak materialism; but there are equally reasonable reservations about whether they have achieved the sort of closure on this issue that they sometimes presume.

(3) *Hylomorphism as dualism*. Of course, these reservations do nothing to show that hylomorphism cannot in the end be construed materialistically. They do, however, show that one cannot immediately rule out the possibility that Aristotle is a dualist, albeit of a markedly non-Platonic sort. Indeed, some texts seem to have just this kind of dualist implication. Accordingly, the initially improbable hypothesis that Aristotle's hylomorphism is best understood as a form of dualism has also found its defenders, among them Robinson (1983), Shields (1988*a*), and Heinaman (1990). Robinson focuses on Aristotle's conception of *nous* as immaterial, chiding other recent scholars for ignor-

ing this feature of Aristotle's thought:[11] 'More often than not nowa-
days the favoured opinion is that Aristotle is essentially or in spirit
some sort of materialist. I say that the favoured opinion is that he is a
materialist *essentially* or *in spirit* because few dare to say that he
actually *is* a materialist, because few dare to deny that his doctrine of
nous is immaterialist' (1983, p. 123). Robinson observes correctly that
the majority of commentators have disregarded Aristotle's conception
of an immaterial *nous*; but he wrongly supposes that all such critical
positions are cavalier. Although there are philosophical questions
about the justifiability of Aristotle's conception of *nous* as immaterial,
Robinson does little to explain or defend Aristotle's position, focusing
instead on the differences he sees between Aristotelian and Cartesian
dualism.[12] Here he sees two principal differences: first, for Aristotle
soul and body 'require each other in a more than purely causal
manner'; second, there are potential differences regarding Cartesian
and Aristotelian conceptions of disembodied existence (1983, pp.
143–4). These differences are hard to make out, and in any case do
nothing to underwrite the plausibility of Aristotle's view, or to address
the understandable philosophical qualms that have led to the scholarly disregard for *nous* which Robinson identifies.[13]

More importantly, in focusing on *nous*, Robinson does not endeav-
our to characterize hylomorphism as such. Thus, even if it is granted
that *nous* is immaterial, this does little to characterize hylomorphism
in any general way. Hylomorphism is a thesis about the relation of
the soul to the body; since for Aristotle the mind is but one capacity
of the soul, an analysis of *nous* provides at most a partial characterization of that thesis.

If we focus on the soul as a whole, a more comprehensive conclusion
may be possible. I have argued, for example, that since the soul is an
individual form, and so a substance, it cannot be an attribute of the
body (Shields 1988*a* and 1988*b*). Moreover, numerous arguments
show that the substantial soul cannot be a magnitude (*megethos*) (see
Shields (1988*a*, §IV)); consequently, Aristotle has strong dualist commitments.[14] At the same time, materialist interpretations like Charles's
are not completely off the mark, since they rightly stress that for
Aristotle mental states (excepting noetic states) supervene on physical
states. These various commitments may strain against one another,
but they are consistent: Aristotle may be a 'supervenient dualist',[15]
who recognizes that anti-reductivism in the philosophy of mind
carries no commitment to robust, Platonic dualism.

Such a dualistic interpretation admits of many exegetical challenges, and certainly questions remain about its tenability. First, merely to say that Aristotle's hylomorphism is consistent may seem faint praise. But here Sorabji's impulse for regarding Aristotle as *sui generis* becomes relevant. If there are no successful strategies for reducing mental properties to physical properties, then we may seem saddled with the equally unattractive alternatives of eliminative materialism and Platonic dualism. Aristotle's point of view introduces subtlety by distinguishing conceptual from ontological separability: souls may depend on bodies for their existence even if mental properties are not reducible to physical properties. Hence, supervenient dualism shares in common with weak materialism the thought that Aristotelian hylomorphism provides a way of recognizing subtle discriminations among views in the philosophy of mind which are often unnecessarily polarized, and wrongly taken to be exhaustive. In this sense, the gulf between the competing formulations of hylomorphism under consideration may not be as wide as would at first appear: all coalesce around the weakest forms of materialism and dualism, and all recognize Aristotle's somewhat elusive perspective as yielding a viable alternative to some more familiar options.

(4) *Hylomorphism and the functionalism debate.* The conflicting signals one finds in the *De Anima* and related psychological treatises go some way toward explaining the arresting divergence of scholarly opinion about hylomorphism. The challenging unclarity of Aristotle's opinions by itself assures the lively scholarly controversy surveyed thus far. But the drive to characterize and understand Aristotle's hylomorphism has also been propelled by recent developments in the philosophy of mind that are quite independent of the history of Aristotelian scholarship. Observing that mental states are in principle multiply realizable,[16] Putnam (1975) came to appreciate that any form of the identity theory, according to which mental-state types are identical with physical-state types, must be false. Even if some version of ontological materialism is correct, one must allow that all mental-state types might be realized by distinct sorts of physical-state types. This reflection led Putnam to take a cue from Aristotle: '. . . what we are really interested in, as Aristotle saw [*DA* 412^{a}6–^{b}6], is form and not matter. *What is our intellectual form?* is the question, not what the matter is. And whatever our substance may be, soul-stuff, or matter or Swiss cheese, it is not going to place any interesting restrictions on

the answer to this question' (1975, p. 302; Putnam's italics). Developing this Aristotelian insight, Putnam propounded a variety of functionalism, according to which mental-state types are to be identified with functional-state types, which in turn are identified by the relations they bear to a system's inputs, outputs, and other mental states. Such functional properties may be realized by physical systems; in humans a given neural state n has the property of being a belief just because it plays a certain functional role.

While contemporary functionalists touted Aristotle as one of their own, scholars began investigating the degree to which such a characterization was accurate. Here again, the verdict is widely divided. Some have seen Aristotle as a thoroughgoing functionalist (Nussbaum and Putnam (1992), Irwin (1991), Shields (1990), Wedin (1988)); others offered qualified rejections (Modrak (1987) and Hartman (1977)); and still others sought to show that Aristotle's view positively precludes rather than sustains a functionalist analysis (Robinson (1978), Granger (1990), Heinaman (1990, §III)).

Among those rejecting a functionalist interpretation, Robinson (1978) has been the most vehement. He offers a series of objections intended to show that even though Aristotle holds that 'every biological process has a function which explains why it exists', he has no interest in providing a 'reductive account of the experience, feeling, or sensation of (e.g.) pain' (1978, p. 111). This worry is a bit obscure. Functionalism has seemed attractive to many precisely because of its *anti*-reductive credentials. Presumably Robinson understands functionalist definitions to be reductive in the sense that they make no essential reference to *qualia*. If so, his characterization of functionalism is apt, but finds no support in the texts of Aristotle. Indeed, in the very passages where Aristotle urges functional definitions as appropriate, one finds no mention of the qualitative character of mental states. Thus, at *De Anima* 403ª26–7 he argues that anger is 'a certain sort of motion of such and such a body, or part or faculty [of a body], by this on account of that'. Amplified, Aristotle's point is that anger is a particular sort of movement with a particular sort of cause and for the sake of a certain end. He neither mentions the qualitative character of anger nor denies that anger has such a character. It is therefore difficult to commit Aristotle to the view that mental states have an *essentially* qualitative character which necessarily eludes functional definition.[17] Hence, Robinson provides no convincing grounds for dismissing functionalist interpretations.[18]

167

Commentators more sympathetic to functionalist interpretations (e.g. Irwin (1991)) have attempted to situate Aristotle's views within his broader teleological framework, in some cases relying on Aristotle's general analysis of kind-identification and -membership (Shields (1990)). Aristotle claims in the *Meteorologica*, for example:

> All things are defined by their function: for [in those cases where] things are able to perform their function, each thing truly is [*F*], for example, an eye, when it can see. But when something cannot [perform that function], it is homonymously [*F*], like a dead eye or one made of stone, just as a wooden saw is no more a saw than one in a picture. ($390^a10{-}15$)

Aristotle asserts that something belongs to a kind *F* just in case it can perform the function definitive of that kind. However unlikely this may seem as an analysis of kind-membership, one consequence would appear to be, for example, that whatever—and only whatever—has the power to see will be an eye; similarly, whatever—and only whatever—can think will be a mind. In allowing that a sufficient condition for belonging to the class of minds is the capacity to think, Aristotle commits himself in principle to the claim that the material constitution of a thing will not place any 'interesting restrictions', as Putnam says, on our account of mind. Consequently, Aristotle apparently endorses a form of compositional plasticity for mental states, and thus recognizes and affirms one central functionalist insight.[19]

This much shows only that a weak form of functionalism is congenial to Aristotle, not that he embraces any articulated version of that view. Still, functionalist interpreters have found significant textual support (e.g., in addition to passages already cited, *DA* $408^b21{-}3$, $414^a19{-}27$; *Meta.* $1036^a31{-}^b7$; *De Part. Anim.* $647^a10{-}12$; *Rhet.* 1378^a31), and have not unreasonably sought to understand hylomorphism from that perspective. We might regard it as one among other welcome consequences of this approach that it helps explain Aristotle's frustratingly non-committal attitude toward some key issues in the ontology of mind. Certainly a functionalist, as such, may prefer to remain aloof in a debate between materialists and dualists: functionalism is equally compatible with either of these views. Aristotle's preference for holding some of these issues in abeyance in the *De Anima* may, then, reflect his recognition that a functionalist version of hylomorphism by itself entails neither materialism nor dualism. Hence, the difficulties one encounters in attempting to show decisively that Aristotle is a weak materialist or a weak, non-Platonic dualist may derive precisely from an overarching commitment to functionalism. He can certainly embrace weak materialism as a functionalist; or if, as suggested, his general characterization of form prohibits him from accepting weak materialism, Aristotle may nevertheless be a functionalist who independently favours a form of supervenient dualism.

(5) *Challenges to hylomorphism.* The drive to characterize Aristotle's hylomorphism and its functionalist commitments is in large measure simply an attempt to unpack and understand his philosophical proposal. This project is fuelled in part, of course, by the hope that Aristotle's hylomorphism may still prove philosophically enlightening. Two significant philosophical challenges call the worth of Aristotle's philosophical programme into serious question. Both Ackrill (1972–3/ 1979) and Burnyeat (1992) have offered arguments which seek to identify fundamental problems in Aristotle's hylomorphism,[20] problems which, if genuine, render a large portion of the reassessment of Aristotle's view philosophically moot. If correct, Ackrill and Burnyeat show how Aristotle's hylomorphic project in the philosophy of mind is a non-starter.

Ackrill argues with great care that Aristotle's application of the form/matter distinction to soul–body relations is altogether infelicitous. Burnyeat follows Ackrill, but offers additional considerations intended to yield the more strident conclusion that Aristotle's philosophy of mind is no longer credible, but should be 'junked' and left to rot with the remaining conceptual flotsam of pre-Cartesian mental philosophy. I shall focus on Ackrill's argument, since the response I offer holds for the core of Burnyeat's as well.[21]

We can understand Aristotle's claim that a bronze statue is a compound of form and matter: when a lump of bronze acquires a particular shape, say the shape of Harmodios, we have a statue of Harmodios. That same quantity of bronze can lose its Harmodios-shape, and acquire another, distinct shape, say the shape of Aristogeiton. The quantity of bronze remains the same, and thus is neither essentially Harmodios- nor Aristogeiton-shaped. The same cannot, however, be said in the case of the soul, since Aristotle contends that the body is homonymous (DA 412^{b}20–5, 412^{b}27–413^{a}2); he suggests, in fact, that a dead body is not a body *except* homonymously (*plēn homōnumōs*).[22] This claim entails that a human body is a human body only when it is ensouled, with the result that human bodies, unlike quantities of bronze, are *essentially* enformed. Ackrill summarizes his point:

> ... Aristotle's definitions of *psuchē* resist interpretation because (i) the contrast of form and matter in a composite makes ready sense only where the matter can be picked out in such a way that it could be conceived as existing without the form, but (ii) his account of body and bodily organs makes unintelligible, given the homonymy principle, the suggestion that this body or these organs might have lacked a *psuchē*. The complaint is not that Aristotle's concept of matter and form commits him to the impossible notion that what has form must lack it—that the same matter both has and has not the form; but that it commits him to something that he cannot allow to be possible in the case of living beings, namely that what has the form might have lacked it—that the same matter has and might not have had the form. (1972–3, p. 70)

Ackrill rightly observes that a commitment to homonymy introduces a salient disanalogy between Aristotle's prime examples of hylomorphic artefacts, e.g. bronze statues, and ensouled bodies. A bronze statue is contingently enformed by the shape it has; bodies are necessarily ensouled. Hence, whereas an enformed mass of bronze will have modal properties at a given time which its correlative form lacks, this will not be the case for living bodies. Thus, Aristotle's calculated tripartite analogy:

form : matter :: Hermes shape : bronze :: soul : body

breaks down: human bodies cannot remain bodies after losing their forms.

In light of this disanalogy, Aristotle might be advised simply to rescind his application of the homonymy principle to human bodies. He needs, evidently, to allow that bodies are contingently enformed, but as Ackrill rightly notes, the homonymy principle undercuts this claim by making bodies necessarily ensouled.

Aristotle cannot take up this advice, at least not without rethinking some central features of his account of kind-membership. If, as the passage from *Meteorologica* IV quoted above suggests, a necessary condition of being a human body is having the capacity to engage in the activities characteristic of human bodies, then corpses cannot be regarded as human bodies, except by custom or courtesy. They lack the determinative capacity. Hence, Aristotle is right to apply the homonymy principle in just the way he does, and is not at liberty simply to withdraw it in light of the disanalogy Ackrill points out. Consequently, Ackrill's argument presents a serious threat to Aristotle's hylomorphism.

To the extent that those engaged in the project of characterizing Aristotle's hylomorphism are unwilling to concede that his views are incoherent, it is incumbent upon them to respond to Ackrill's argument. Several, including Cohen (1987), Whiting (1992), and Shields (1993), have defended hylomorphism against Ackrill's charge. The strongest reply is in some ways initially concessive. Ackrill is correct in maintaining that the homonymy principle entails that human bodies are essentially ensouled. Even so, Aristotle distinguishes two sorts of human bodies, organic and non-organic. After defining the soul as the 'form of a body having life in potentiality' (*eidos sōmatos phusikou dunamei zōēn echontos*, *DA* 412ª19–20), Aristotle adds at 412ª28–ᵇ1 'this sort of body would be one which is organic' (*toiouton de ho an ēi organikon*). Aristotle never characterizes by name the body which is not organic; still, he draws a distinction which implies its existence. This distinction between the organic and the non-organic body allows him to avoid contradiction. He can satisfy the homonymy principle by holding that the *organic* human body is necessarily ensouled, and the demands of hylomorphism by holding that the non-organic human body is contingently ensouled. A non-organic body can then survive the destruction of the compound in the same way that a quantity of bronze persists through the destruction of a statue of Harmodios. Consequently, Aristotle can acknowledge the plain fact that a human body of some sort survives the instant of death, and can therefore justifiably describe, as he does, a human body which has lost or 'thrown off' (*apobeblēkos*) its soul at the organism's death (*DA* 412ᵇ25).

This line of response to Ackrill's argument is promising, but invites some attendant difficulties of its own. For example, it becomes necessary to characterize the complex relation between the organic and non-organic body, as well as the relation between these and the soul, in what looks to become a fairly cluttered theory.[23] Organic and non-organic bodies cannot be identical, since in that case the one could not be essentially and the other only contingently ensouled. Moreover, in his definition of the soul, Aristotle characterizes organic bodies as *potentially* alive, rather than as actually alive (*DA* 412ª19–21, 27–8).

But the response sketched concedes to Ackrill that some body, namely the organic body, is not only actually alive, but *necessarily* actually alive. Yet we normally speak of something's being potentially *F* only when it is not actually *F*. (When asked if Wellington led the British forces at Waterloo, one would be perverse to answer, 'Yes, potentially.') Hence, either Aristotle contradicts himself, or it is possible for him to hold that some things are both potentially and actually *F*. His analysis of actuality and potentiality suggests such a possibility;[24] but it should be clear that Ackrill's argument poses some far-reaching challenges to the defenders of hylomorphism.

III

Aristotle marks off distinct psychic faculties. The broadest, the ability to take in nutrition, is shared by all living things, including plants, which are consequently ensouled. In addition to this capacity, animals have perception (*aisthēsis*), while human beings have mind (*nous*) as well. The status of imagination (*phantasia*), to which Aristotle devotes a chapter of the *De Anima*, is somewhat in doubt. Aristotle distinguishes it from both reason (*dianoia*) and perception (*DA* 427^b14; cf. 428^a17ff.), while connecting it intimately to both perception (*DA* 425^b25; cf. 427^b15, 428^b11ff.) and thinking (*noēsis*: *DA* 433^a10). Moreover, animals and human beings equally have imagination; but it is not clear whether they have the same type, since Aristotle distinguishes rational from perceptual imagination (*DA* 433^b29–434^a5). In any case, as Kahn notes (1966/1979, pp. 4–5, with n. 17), Aristotle divides his treatment of these various capacities unevenly, giving the lion's share to perception.[25]

(1) *Perception*. Although Aristotle deals with perception (*aisthēsis*) and the individual senses in some detail, he does little to characterize the faculty in any general way. Modrak (1981) investigates Aristotle's analysis of perception, and seeks to reconstruct the theoretical substructure underlying his account. She argues that a unified and largely defensible theoretical framework underpins Aristotle's sometimes seemingly disparate characterizations of sensory activity.

Among the principles Modrak attributes to Aristotle[26] is what she calls the Actuality Principle: a cognitive faculty is potentially what its object is actually. Aristotle clearly holds some such view, but it is difficult to determine his meaning precisely. He says: 'that which can

perceive is potentially such as the object of sense already is actually'
(*DA* 418ᵃ3–4). He cannot think that the sensory faculty and the
object of sense become numerically identical;²⁷ he must hold, as he
goes on to clarify, that these become one in form (*DA* 431ᵇ29; cf.
429ᵃ13–18). But the import of this claim is unclear.²⁸ For example,
does Aristotle think that the sense organs are receptive of sensible
qualities in such a way that they actually manifest those qualities, so
that, for example, the eye becomes red when perceiving a red object?
Sorabji affirms that he does (1974/1979; see also 1971/1979, pp. 78–
9). This claim is doubtful, and it must in any case be appreciated that
it admits of a stronger and a weaker formulation. Aristotle might
hold, mistakenly as Philoponus already pointed out (*In De Anima*, p.
303, lines 3 ff.), that *aisthēsis* can occur only if the relevant sense organ
actually takes on the quality being perceived. Or he might hold more
strongly that *aisthēsis* just consists in this physiological process. Nothing
in the *De Anima* grounds the stronger claim; on the contrary, *DA* 424ᵇ16–
18 suggests just the opposite.²⁹ Hence, there is no reason to think that, for
example, the coloration of the eye jelly constitutes a given act of seeing.
This being so, the weaker thesis, that this sort of coloration is necessary for
perception, loses much of its interest. Although clearly interested in
the physiology of perception (*DA* 403ᵃ25–ᵇ9), Aristotle does not
suppose that there is nothing to say about *aisthēsis* beyond the false
and unilluminating view that the sense organs always manifest the
qualities they perceive.³⁰ Still, Sorabji provides *an* account that makes
literal sense of Aristotle's contention that the sensory faculties are
potentially what their objects are actually, a claim that has otherwise
proven remarkably difficult to unpack, let alone defend.³¹

Corresponding to Aristotle's claim that the senses are potentially
what their objects are actually is his view that the sensory faculties
are related as such (*kath' hauto*) to their objects. In holding such a
view, Aristotle evidently suggests that a given faculty is defined or at
least individuated by its objects,³² and as a methodological correlate
that one must explicate sense objects in order to understand sensory
faculties. Aristotle respects the proposed methodology in his discussions of the individual senses,³³ as well as in his discussion of incidental
perception (on which see Cashdollar (1973)) and the common sense
(on which see Modrak (1981) and Block (1988)).

(2) *Imagination*. It is less clear whether Aristotle respects this proposed
methodology for imagination (*phantasia*). Aristotle considers imagina-

tion principally in *De Anima* III. 3, a transitional chapter bridging his discussions of perception and mind, and one fraught with textual problems and seeming incongruities. Unfortunately, Aristotle does little to characterize imagination in any positive way. Although he does say, rather narrowly, that imagination is 'that in virtue of which an image occurs in us' ($430^{a}1$–2), the bulk of this chapter is given over to differentiating imagination from other faculties of the soul. In the process of doing so, Aristotle relies on partial characterizations of the faculties he seeks to distinguish and sometimes ignores distinctions drawn elsewhere in the *De Anima*. For example, Aristotle once differentiates imagination from perception on the ground that some animals have perception without imagination, even though he later recognizes two forms of imagination, one, a deliberative form, available to human beings, while the other, perceptive imagination, is 'found in the other animals' (*DA* $434^{a}6$–7). This is not a contradiction, since Aristotle might hold that perceptive imagination extends to some but not all animals (this indeed seems to be his view at *DA* $428^{a}9$–11; but cf. *Meta.* $980^{b}22$ and *De Part. Anim.* $648^{a}5$). Even so, the tensions of the chapter initially support Hamlyn's finding: 'there is clearly little consistency here' (see his note to *DA* 427^{b}).

Several scholars have sought ways to overcome seeming deficiencies of Aristotle's account of imagination. Schofield (1978/1979) considers the role *phantasia* plays in Aristotle's philosophy of mind, and argues that 'the range of phenomena Aristotle assigns to *phantasia* . . . suggests a rather different physiognomy for the concept from that conveyed by "imagination"' (p. 106; but cf. second thoughts on p. 107); rather, Aristotle is concerned with a psychic capacity for handling 'non-paradigmatic sensory experiences' (p. 106). On this account, Aristotle's conception of *phantasia* is not so much inconsistent or underdeveloped as so pervasive that it encompasses many disparate forms of experience (for instance, dreaming, or puzzling out an indistinct image), each of which resembles—but is not—a paradigmatic instance of sense perception. Thus, imagination for Aristotle is a sort of residual faculty dedicated to housing a set of quasi-sensory experiences related to one another at best by family resemblances.

Wedin (1988, e.g. at pp. 24, 65–7) is critical of Schofield's account. He rightly points out that Aristotle allows images to accompany paradigmatic sensory experience at *DA* $428^{b}25$–30, and thus connects imagination and sense perception in ways inimical to Schofield's approach (for the latter's concessive comments on this passage, see

Schofield (1978/1979, p. 118)). Wedin argues instead that imagination is a 'creature of theory . . . [which] yields a surprisingly sophisticated theory of [re]presentational[34] structures within an essentially functionalist framework' (p. 24). Wedin attributes some of the problems Aristotle's commentators have located in his account of imagination to a misunderstanding of its true status: he somewhat perplexingly seeks to show that imagination is not a full-blown Aristotelian capacity, but is instead a sort of sub-faculty working in concert with the fully developed capacities of perception and mind (1988, pp. 45–63, 254). The advantages of this approach are unclear. One question concerns what is gained by regarding imagination as incomplete; another concerns the plausibility of this view in light of Aristotle's typically treating imagination as on par with the other faculties (e.g. at 414^b33–415^b3); and yet another concerns Aristotle's identifying objects of imagination in the same ways that he identifies objects of sense perception and mind (at *De Memoria* 450^a24; for Wedin's assessment, see his pp. 61–3). Still, Wedin offers a sophisticated and novel approach to Aristotle's conception, and provides astute commentary on many of the individual passages in which Aristotle discusses imagination.[35]

(3) *Mind.* Aristotle opens *DA* III. 4 by describing mind (*nous*) as 'the part of the soul by which it [the soul] knows and understands' (*DA* 429^a9–10). Like the perceptive capacity of the soul, the mind thinks by receiving the forms of its objects (*DA* 429^a13–18).[36] But unlike the perceptive faculty, *nous* lacks an organ, a thesis Aristotle seeks to infer from the sort of plasticity required for thinking a broad range of objects (*DA* 429^a29–$^b9$). Commentators often presume that Aristotle's argument for the immateriality of *nous* rests essentially on the impoverished empirical science of his day. In consequence, many agree with Hartman in holding that 'Aristotle's doctrine of *nous* is a weak spot in an otherwise plausible and well-argued theory of mental entities and events' (1977, p. 7). Yet many who disparage Aristotle's dualism find his account of thinking and intentionality worth pursuing.[37]

For example, Wedin (1986 and 1988) finds instructive parallels between Aristotle's views and a contemporary position he labels 'cognitivism', and in this context advances a number of theses about *nous* worth investigating. Especially noteworthy is his treatment of the active mind (*nous poiētikos*) introduced in *De Anima* III. 5. In working to establish a clear function for *nous poiētikos*, Wedin usefully stresses the role this faculty plays in Aristotle's account of the autonomy of human cognition. Although his relentlessly naturalistic interpretation of *nous poiētikos* cuts against the grain of the text,[38] Wedin provides ample reason to reject Hartman's view that Aristotle's account of *nous poiētikos* 'is an inadequate answer to a wrongheaded question' (1977, p. 221). On Wedin's approach, *nous poiētikos* has a role to play both in the acquisition of concepts and in the movement from dispositional to occurrent knowledge which occurs when, for example, someone who knows the paradox generated by the Russell set, but is not occupied with it, calls it forth into consciousness. Aristotle rightly acknowledges that one can know in these different senses (*DA* 412^{a}22–3), and embeds his account in his general distinction between types of actuality (417^{a}21–418^{a}6; cf. *Phys.* 255^{a}30–^{b}5). It is a virtue of Wedin's analysis that it provides Aristotle with a mechanism which at least partially explains these distinct types of actualizations (1988, p. 254); even so, as Wedin acknowledges, some features of the autonomy of thinking presupposed in Aristotle's distinction resist clear explication, even granting *nous poiētikos* this role.

IV

This brief overview has, of necessity, omitted mention of many valuable scholarly works. But perhaps the general outlines I have sketched give at least a faint indication of the liveliness and quality that have characterized recent discussion of Aristotle's *De Anima*. Even where consensus has been lacking, progress has been possible; and such disagreement as persists is as often a sign of health as it is of scholarly disarray. The *De Anima* continues to offer various exegetical puzzles and obstacles to philosophical closure. Even so, the redoubtable theory it propounds fully deserves the scrutiny it has inspired.[39]

NOTES

1. Lawson-Tancred (1986) follows Sorabji in regarding hylomorphism as *sui generis*, though his argument proceeds along a different track.
2. Nussbaum (1984, p. 206) urges this as a benefit of Aristotle's hylomorphism.

3. Sorabji here concurs with Wiggins (1971) and Ackrill (1972–3/ 1979) in seeing the notion of constitution as playing a central role in Aristotle's approach.

4. Barnes claims: 'ϕ is physical if ϕ is definable in terms of the primitive predicates of physics (and, if necessary, of chemistry; and, if necessary, of biology)' (1971–2/1979, p. 34). Weak physicalism, in Barnes's sense, should therefore be regarded as a species of what I have called weak materialism: it adds to the claim that token mental states are also token physical states the further claim that psychological predicates can perhaps be reduced to the primitive predicates of physics, or at least to chemistry or biology. In the text I argue that Barnes's argument fails to establish weak materialism; if this is correct, it trivially fails to establish weak physicalism. This is a point of some interest since even if Aristotle is a materialist, there will remain the further question of whether he supposes that mental properties can be reduced (e.g. via supervenient bridge laws) to physical properties.

5. NB that there is some tension in Barnes's view insofar as he does not think that Aristotle is a weak physicalist *tout court*. Rather, after arguing that non-separability entails physicalism, he concedes that Aristotle nevertheless endorses non-physicalism for some capacities of the soul, notably mind and perhaps the desiderative capacity. He accordingly concludes that Aristotle 'emerges as a fairly consistent upholder of an attribute theory of mind' (1971–2/1979, p. 41). Shields (1988a, §III) reviews and rejects Barnes's suggestion that hylomorphism is a version of the attribute theory.

6. The question of whether Aristotelian forms are particular as well as universal has received a great deal of attention since Hamlyn. This literature touches upon the question of hylomorphism precisely because the soul is a form, and evidently a particular. Frede (1978/1987, pp. 68–9) considers this issue; for a fuller discussion, see Sellars (1957).

7. Even a dualist who thought that mental states supervened on physical states could endorse Charles's 'ontological materialism'. Consequently, Charles's interpretation, while certainly compatible with materialism, does not actually require that all psychological states be physical states; and this would seem to be necessary for any recognizably materialist view. Charles seems to want to

hold that so long as the relevant bodily sufficiency is non-causal, Aristotle is committed to ontological materialism; if so, he overlooks the form of non-causal nomological sufficiency required by supervenience relations.

8. For a discussion of the connate pneuma, see Nussbaum (1978, pp. 143–64).

9. Indeed, if Aristotle had intended principle (PC) in this passage, then he would have contradicted himself, since he equally holds that his unmoved mover is a source of movement, an *archē tēs kinēseōs*, which, as Ross notes, is simply Aristotle's Greek for 'efficient cause' (*Metaphysics*, ed. W. D. Ross, vol. i., p. cxxxiv). Agreeing with Charles that an efficient cause is an antecedent sufficient condition, a commitment to (PC) in the *De Motu Animalium* would commit Aristotle to the view that there could not be the immaterial antecedent sufficient causes of motion he elsewhere recognizes.

10. For further discussion and criticism of Charles (1984) on this point, see Heinaman (1990, pp. 98–9).

11. He cites Wilkes (1978, pp. 115–16), Nussbaum (1978, pp. 267–8), and Hartman (1977, pp. 6–7, 221).

12. For our purposes it will suffice to identify Cartesian dualism with Platonic dualism, in the sense specified.

13. Nussbaum (1984) responds to Robinson, by suggesting that *DA* 412^{b}6–9 not only precludes dualism but 'forestalls the whole Cartesian question. It says, don't ask that question. And it says you won't ask if you have attended in the appropriate way to the complex materiality of living things' (p. 206).

14. Heinaman (1990, p. 84; cf. p. 85 n. 5) doubts this last inference, since he holds that a materialist can regard certain properties, e.g. shapes, as not constituted by matter without abandoning her materialism. This is of course true, since properties, if there are properties, are abstract entities, and no materialist rejects materialism by endorsing realism about universals. But on the account advanced in Shields (1988*a*), the soul is not a universal; it is rather an immaterial particular.

15. Shields (1988*a*) explicitly attributes supervenient dualism to Aristotle; Heinaman offers him a similar view, holding first that he is a dualist, and second that 'the soul is a *dynamis* that supervenes (*epigignetai*) on the body when the organization of matter has reached a certain level' (1990, p. 90; cf. p. 91).

16. This is just the thought that one and the same mental-state type can be realized in different physical systems: thus pain is realized in one way in humans and another in dogs; the belief that dogs have pain is realized in one way in humans and (in principle) in another way in Martians. For comparison: the same function, say of adding two with two, can be realized in calculators composed of different stuffs and in different configurations.

17. It is further to be noted that functionalism does not entail that mental states have no qualitative character; it just does not regard this as a defining feature. Moreover, *qualia* may yet admit of functional definitions, at least insofar as second-order qualitative beliefs may necessarily accompany all qualitative states. If so, then Robinson's reservations are still less well motivated: Aristotle may admit, as he should, that mental states have qualitative character without *ipso facto* rejecting functionalism. So the thesis that Aristotle is a functionalist is in no way undermined by the existence of *qualia*.

18. Robinson provides a host of additional arguments. For discussion and replies, see Shields (1990, p. 32 n. 21).

19. For doubts about this claim, see Heinaman (1990, p. 100).

20. See also Williams (1986), who follows Ackrill (1972–3/1979) for the most part, but who also teases out in greater detail some of the initially counter-intuitive consequences of Aristotle's hylomorphism.

21. For a discussion of Burnyeat, see Cohen (1987).

22. For Aristotle's conception of the body as homonymous, see Cohen (1987), Shields (1993), and Whiting (1992).

23. Shields (1993) offers a first approximation of an approach available to Aristotle.

24. Whiting (1992, §III) develops this line.

25. The divisions are not as clean as this list suggests, but the faculties are treated roughly as follows: nutrition, *DA* II. 4; perception, *DA* II. 5–12 and III. 1–2; imagination, *DA* III. 3; mind, *DA* III. 4–5. Thus Aristotle treats perception in ten Bekker pages, mind in three, and the remaining capacities in four.

26. She identifies altogether five theoretical presuppositions, three substantive and two methodological (p. 51, ch. 2). In addition to the Actuality Principle, the substantive theses are: (i) the Psychophysical Principle: most psychic states are psychophysical, that is, physically realized states of the soul; (ii) the Sensory Representa-

tion Principle: whenever a cognitive activity has a sense object as its focal object, the operative psychic faculty is the perceptual faculty. The methodological theses are: (*a*) The Analytic Principle: psychological explanations should begin by explicating the constituent parts of psychic phenomena; and (*b*) the Normative Psychophysical Principle: given principle (i), any comprehensive psychological theory will address the psychophysical character of psychological states. In relying primarily on *De Anima* 403ª16–18 and *De Sensu* 436ª7–10, Modrak does not clearly establish (i), and so provides no basis for (*b*). In these passages Aristotle notes that sensation involves the body, but falls short of claiming that sensation is *essentially* a physical process.

27. This seems to be the purport of Lear (1988, pp. 125, 131; but cf. pp. 134, 140).

28. See Bernard (1988, pp. 49–68) for a clear and persuasive discussion of this claim in the context of *De Anima* II. 5. Bernard's book provides close and illuminating commentary on many passages concerning Aristotle's theory of perception.

29. See Heinaman (1990, pp. 97–8).

30. See Kosman (1975) and Modrak (1987, pp. 58–9 with p. 199 n. 15).

31. Slakey (1961) investigates the question whether this contention admits of a defensible interpretation, and offers a negative verdict.

32. Hamlyn (1959) has doubted this construal of Aristotle's view, urging instead that his point runs in the other direction, so that sense objects are defined by their correlative capacities. Sorabji (1971/1979) overcomes Hamlyn's reservations.

33. Sorabji defends this approach with the exception of touch (1971/1979, pp. 85–92).

34. The brackets in '[re]presentational' are Wedin's. He employs this device to avoid 'foisting on Aristotle the view that we do not actually perceive objects but only make inferences to them from Hume-like images' (1988, p. 17 n. 27).

35. For a more narrow textual commentary, see Rees (1971), and for an assessment of Aristotle's account of imagination in relation to Plato's and to some contemporary accounts, see Lycos (1964).

36. Lowe (1983) argues that Aristotle never assimilates thinking to perception, and indeed that one major aim of his discussion of thinking is precisely to determine how sensation and thinking are

distinct. He seeks to show that Aristotle distinguishes between types of thinking which have no clear parallels in sensation: apprehensive thinking, which concerns objects of thought with matter, and autonomous thinking, which concerns objects without matter. He locates a further disanalogy in Aristotle's distinction between fallible and infallible thinking in *DA* III. 6.

37. Of special interest to Aristotle's English-language readers is the appearance of a translation of Brentano's classic study *Die Psychologie des Aristoteles* (1867/1977). Although he both interprets and appropriates Aristotle's account of thinking in fertile ways, Brentano's discussions have been somewhat neglected. This may in part be due to the idiosyncratic character of his lively, developmental exegesis; however that may be, his discussions are philosophically animated, and engage Aristotle's texts so as to display the richness his framework holds for dealing with problems in intentionality. To see that this is so, one may consult Brentano's account of Aristotle's insistence that *nous* lacks an organ. As suggested, it is easy to interpret Aristotle's claim that mind cannot be mixed with the body as resulting from a narrow empirical shortcoming: Aristotle sought in vain to locate an organ of thought, and so inferred that the mind must be immaterial. In Brentano's hands (pp. 80–2), the argument is far subtler.

38. See Rist (1966) for a close account of *De Anima* III. 5. See also Hardie (1980, ch. 16). Perhaps the fullest discussion is Brentano (1867/1977). Brentano's succinct review of pre-twentieth-century views has been excerpted from Brentano (1867/1977) and published separately as Brentano (1992).

39. Many people have been kind enough to read drafts of this report. For detailed written remarks, I thank: J. Anderson, T. Irwin, N. Kretzmann, S. MacDonald, and P. Mitsis. I am specially thankful to L. Judson and J. Ackrill for their keen and abundant advice at every stage of this project.

BIBLIOGRAPHY

TRANSLATIONS AND COMMENTARIES

APOSTLE, HIPPOCRATES (1981), *Aristotle's On the Soul* (Grinell, Iowa: Peripatetic Press).

HETT, W. S. (1957), *Aristotle: On the Soul, etc.* (Loeb Classical Library; Cambridge, Mass.: Harvard University Press.)

HICKS, R. D. (1907), *Aristotle: De Anima* (Cambridge: Cambridge University Press).

JANNONE, A., and BARBOTIN, E. (1966), *Aristote: De l'âme* (Paris: Budé).

LAWSON-TANCRED, HUGH (1986), *Aristotle: De Anima* (Harmondsworth: Penguin).

RODIER, G. (1900), *Aristote: Traité de l'âme* (Paris: Leroux).

ROSS, W. D. (1961), *Aristotle: De Anima* (Oxford: Clarendon Press).

SIWEK, P. (1965), *Aristotelis tractatus de anima, graece et latine* (Rome: Desclée).

SMITH, J. A. (1984), *De Anima*, in *The Collected Works of Aristotle*, ed. J. Barnes (Princeton: Princeton University Press), 641–92.

THEILER, W. (1979), *Aristoteles: Über die Seele* (Berlin: Akademie Verlag).

ARTICLES AND BOOKS

ACKRILL, J. L. (1965), 'Aristotle's Distinction between *Energeia* and *Kinesis*', in *New Essays on Plato and Aristotle*, ed. R. Bambrough (London: Routledge & Kegan Paul), 121–42.

—— (1972–3), 'Aristotle's Definitions of *Psuchē*', *Proceedings of the Aristotelian Society*, LXXIII: 119–33; reprinted in Barnes *et al.* (1979), 65–75. All references are to the latter pagination.

BARNES, JONATHAN (1971–2), 'Aristotle's Concept of Mind', *Proceedings of the Aristotelian Society*, LXXII: 101–10; reprinted in Barnes *et al.* (1979), 32–41. All references are to the latter pagination.

——SCHOFIELD, M., and SORABJI, R., edd. (1979), *Articles on Aristotle* (New York: St Martin's Press), vol. 4.

BIBLIOGRAPHY

BEARE, J. I. (1906), *Greek Theories of Elementary Cognition* (Oxford: Clarendon Press).

BERNARD, WOLFGANG (1988), *Rezeptivität und Spontaneität der Wahrnehmung bei Aristoteles* (Baden-Baden: Verlag Valentin Koerner).

BERTI, ENRICO (1978), 'The Intellection of "Indivisibles" according to Aristotle: *De Anima* III. 6', in *Aristotle on Mind and the Senses*, ed. G. E. R. Lloyd and G. E. L. Owen (Cambridge: Cambridge University Press), 141–63.

BLOCK, IRVING (1960–1), 'Aristotle and the Physical Object', *Philosophy and Phenomenological Research*, 21: 93–101.

—— (1961*a*), 'Truth and Error in Aristotle's Theory of Sense Perception', *Philosophical Quarterly*, 11: 1–9.

—— (1961*b*), 'The Order of Aristotle's Psychological Writings', *American Journal of Philology*, 82: 50–77.

—— (1964), 'Three German Commentators on the Individual Senses and the Common Sense in Aristotle', *Phronesis*, 9: 58–63.

—— (1988), 'Aristotle on the Common Sense: A Reply to Kahn and Others', *Ancient Philosophy*, 8: 235–49.

BOLTON, ROBERT (1978), 'Aristotle's Definitions of the Soul: *De Anima* II, 1–3', *Phronesis*, 23: 258–78.

BRENTANO, FRANZ (1867/1977), *Die Psychologie des Aristoteles* (Mainz: Kirchheim); translated by R. George as *The Psychology of Aristotle* (Berkeley: University of California Press, 1977). References are to the translation.

—— (1992), '*Nous Poiētikos*: Survey of Earlier Interpretations', in *Essays on Aristotle's* De Anima, ed. M. Nussbaum and A. Rorty (Oxford: Clarendon Press), 313–41.

BURNYEAT, MYLES (1992), 'Is Aristotle's Philosophy of Mind Still Credible?', in *Essays on Aristotle's* De Anima, ed. M. Nussbaum and A. Rorty (Oxford: Clarendon Press), 15–26.

CASHDOLLAR, STANFORD (1973), 'Aristotle's Account of Incidental Perception', *Phronesis*, 18: 156–75.

CHARLES, DAVID (1984), *Aristotle's Philosophy of Action* (Ithaca: Cornell University Press).

CHARLTON, WILLIAM (1981), 'Aristotle's Definition of Soul', *Phronesis*, 26: 170–86.

COHEN, S. MARC (1987), 'The Credibility of Aristotle's Philosophy of Mind', in *Aristotle Today: Aristotle's Ideal of Science*, ed. Mohan Matthen (Edmonton, Canada: Academic Printing), 103–25.

FREDE, MICHAEL (1978/1987), 'Individuen bei Aristoteles', *Antike und Abendland*, 24: 16–39; translated by W. Mann as 'Individuals in Aristotle', in *Essays in Ancient Philosophy* (Minneapolis: University of Minnesota Press, 1987), 49–71. References are to the translation.

GRANGER, HERBERT (1990), 'Aristotle and the Functionalism Debate', *Apeiron*, 23: 27–49.

HAMLYN, D. W. (1959), 'Aristotle's Account of Aesthesis in the *De Anima*', *Classical Quarterly*, NS 9: 6–16.

—— (1961), *Sensation and Perception* (London: Routledge).

—— (1965), 'Seeing Things as They Are' (Inaugural Lecture at Birkbeck College), esp. 12–16.

—— (1968), 'Koine Aisthesis', *The Monist*, 52: 195–209.

—— (1978), 'Aristotle's Cartesianism', *Paideia*, Special Aristotle Issue: 8–15.

—— (1985), 'Aristotle on Form', in *Aristotle on Nature and Living Things*, ed. A. Gotthelf (Pittsburgh: Mathesis; Bristol: Bristol Classical Press), 55–65.

—— (1987), 'Aristotle's God', in *The Philosophical Assessment of Theology*, ed. Gerard J. Hughes (Tunbridge Wells: Search Press; Washington, DC: Georgetown University Press), 15–33.

HARDIE, W. F. R. (1964), 'Aristotle's Treatment of the Relation between the Soul and the Body', *Philosophical Quarterly*, 14: 53–72.

—— (1976), 'Concepts of Consciousness in Aristotle', *Mind*, 85: 388–411.

—— (1980), *Aristotle's Ethical Theory*, 2nd edn. (Oxford: Clarendon Press), chs. 5 and 16.

HARTMAN, EDWIN (1977), *Substance, Body and Soul* (Princeton: Princeton University Press).

HEINAMAN, ROBERT (1990), 'Aristotle and the Mind–Body Problem', *Phronesis*, 35: 83–102.

IRWIN, TERENCE (1981), 'Homonymy in Aristotle', *Review of Metaphysics*, 34: 523–44.

—— (1988), *Aristotle's First Principles* (Oxford: Clarendon Press), chs. 12–15.

—— (1991), 'Aristotle's Philosophy of Mind', in *Companion to Ancient Thought: The Philosophy of Mind*, ed. S. Everson (Cambridge: Cambridge University Press), 56–83.

KAHN, CHARLES (1966), 'Sensation and Consciousness in Aristotle's

Psychology', *Archiv für Geschichte der Philosophie*, 48: 43–81; reprinted in Barnes *et al.* (1979), 1–31. All references are to the latter pagination.

KOSMAN, L. A. (1975), 'Perceiving that we Perceive: *On the Soul* III, 2', *Philosophical Review*, 84: 499–519.

LEAR, JONATHAN (1988), *Aristotle: The Desire to Understand* (Cambridge: Cambridge University Press), ch. 4.

LEFÈVRE, C. (1972), *Sur l'évolution d'Aristote en psychologie* (Louvain: Éditions de l'Institut Supérieur de Philosophie).

LOWE, MALCOLM (1983), 'Aristotle on Kinds of Thinking', *Phronesis*, 28: 17–30.

LYCOS, K. (1964), 'Aristotle and Plato on Appearing', *Mind*, NS 73: 496–514.

MANSION, S. (1978), 'Soul and Life in the *De Anima*', in *Aristotle on Mind and the Senses*, ed. G. E. R. Lloyd and G. E. L. Owen (Cambridge: Cambridge University Press), 1–20.

MAUDLIN, TIM (1986), '*De Anima* II 1: Is Any Sense Missing?', *Phronesis*, 31: 51–67.

MODRAK, DEBORAH K. (1981), '*Koine Aisthesis* and the Discrimination of Sensible Differences in *De Anima* III. 2', *Canadian Journal of Philosophy*, 11: 405–23.

—— (1987) *Aristotle: The Power of Perception* (Chicago: University of Chicago Press).

NUSSBAUM, MARTHA C. (1978), *Aristotle's De Motu Animalium* (Princeton: Princeton University Press), essays 3 and 5.

—— (1984), 'Aristotelian Dualism: Reply to Robinson', *Oxford Studies in Ancient Philosophy*, 2: 198–207.

—— and PUTNAM, HILARY (1992), 'Changing Aristotle's Mind', in *Essays on Aristotle's* De Anima, ed. M. Nussbaum and A. Rorty (Oxford: Clarendon Press), 27–56.

NUYENS, F. (1948), *L'Évolution de la psychologie d'Aristote* (Louvain: Éditions de l'Institut Supérieur de Philosophie).

PUTNAM, HILARY (1975), 'Philosophy and Our Mental Life', in *Mind, Language, and Reality* (Cambridge: Cambridge University Press), 291–303.

REES, D. A. (1971), 'Aristotle's Treatment of *Phantasia*', *Essays in Ancient Greek Philosophy*, ed. J. Anton and G. Kustas (Albany, NY: SUNY Press), 491–504.

RIST, J. (1966), 'Notes on Aristotle's *De Anima* 3.5', *Classical Philology*, 61: 8–20.

ROBINSON, H. M. (1978), 'Mind and Body in Aristotle', *Classical Quarterly*, NS 28: 105–24.

——— (1983), 'Aristotelian Dualism', *Oxford Studies in Ancient Philosophy*, 1: 123–44.

SCHOFIELD, MALCOLM (1978), 'Aristotle on the Imagination', in *Aristotle on Mind and the Senses*, ed. G. E. R. Lloyd and G. E. L. Owen (Cambridge: Cambridge University Press), 99–129; reprinted in Barnes *et al.* (1979), 103–32. All references are to the latter pagination.

SELLARS, WILFRED (1957), 'Substance and Form in Aristotle', *Journal of Philosophy*, 54: 470–84.

SHIELDS, CHRISTOPHER (1988*a*), 'Soul and Body in Aristotle', *Oxford Studies in Ancient Philosophy*, 6: 103–37.

——— (1988*b*), 'Soul as Subject in Aristotle's *De Anima*', *Classical Quarterly*, 38: 140–9.

——— (1990), 'The First Functionalist', *Essays on the Historical Foundations of Cognitive Science*, ed. J.-C. Smith (Dordrecht: Kluwer), 19–33.

——— (1993), 'The Homonymy of the Body in Aristotle', *Archiv für Geschichte der Philosophie*.

SLAKEY, THOMAS (1961), 'Aristotle on Sense Perception', *Philosophical Review*, 70: 470–84.

SORABJI, RICHARD (1971), 'Aristotle on Demarcating the Five Senses', *Philosophical Review*, 80: 55–79; reprinted in Barnes *et al.* (1979), 76–92. All references are to the latter pagination.

——— (1974), 'Body and Soul in Aristotle', *Philosophy*, 49: 63–89; reprinted in Barnes *et al.* (1979), 42–64. All references are to the latter pagination.

——— (1982), 'Myths about Non-propositional Thought', in *Language and Logos*, ed. M. Schofield and M. Nussbaum (Cambridge: Cambridge University Press), 295–314.

WEDIN, MICHAEL V. (1986), 'Tracking Aristotle's *Nous*', in *Human Nature and Natural Knowledge*, ed. A. Donagan *et al.* (Dordrecht: Kluwer), 167–97.

——— (1988), *Mind and Imagination in Aristotle* (New Haven: Yale University Press).

——— (1989), 'Aristotle on the Mechanics of Thought', *Ancient Philosophy*, 9: 67–86.

WHITING, JENNIFER (1992), 'Living Bodies', in *Essays on Aristotle's* De Anima, ed. M. Nussbaum and A. Rorty (Oxford: Clarendon Press), 75–92.

WIGGINS, DAVID (1971), *Identity and Spatio-Temporal Continuity* (Oxford: Blackwell).

WILKES, KATHLEEN V. (1978), *Physicalism* (London: Routledge & Kegan Paul).

WILLIAMS, BERNARD (1986), 'Hylomorphism', *Oxford Studies in Ancient Philosophy*, 4: 189–99.

INDEX OF GREEK TERMS
DISCUSSED

GENERAL INDEX

The references in bold type are those to the Translation.

850 H1